Presented to:

_____

From:

_____

I
DECLARE
WAR

BREE VANLEY

ABUNDANT GRACE
PUBLISHING HOUSE

I Declare War

Published in Little Rock, Arkansas by Abundant Grace Publishing House, LLC. For permission requests, contact Abundant Grace Publishing House at www.agphouse.com or info@agphouse.com.

Unless otherwise noted, all Scripture quotations are taken from the *Holy Bible*, New Living Translation, copyright © 1996, 2004, 2015 by Tyndale House Foundation. Used by permission of Tyndale House Publishers, Inc., Carol Stream, Illinois 60188. All rights reserved.

Scripture notations marked ESV are taken from the ESV® Bible (THE HOLY BIBLE, ENGLISH STANDARD VERSION®), copyright © 2001 by Crossway, a publishing ministry of Good News Publishers. Used by permission. All rights reserved.

Unmarked Scripture quotations are the author's paraphrase.

While the events in this publication are true, names have been removed to protect the identities of those involved.

The author has chosen the stylistic preference of not capitalizing certain names such as 'satan', 'asherah', 'dagon', or 'baphomet'.

ISBN-13: 979-8-218-48769-0

Library of Congress Control Number: 2024916386

Printed in the United States of America

This book is dedicated to those who are not afraid to fight back...

CONTENTS

"I had a dream about you. You had a bomb, like a rocket bomb, and you were ready to be launched. And all I could think of was warfare. You were ready to go to war."

– Pastor Tony Gooding, author of *Spirit to Spirit*

INTRODUCTION

My first friend in this world was my oldest brother. As the younger sibling, I naturally wanted to do whatever he did and go wherever he went. I'm sure I annoyed him by doing this, but I would not change my childhood experience for anything. We did quite a few activities together, including playing a game called I Declare War.

This is how we played: one person would shuffle the deck of cards and deal an equal amount to each player. Since there were only two of us playing, we each received 26 cards. They had to be kept face down, without sneaking a peak. Each player would then flip over the first card on their deck and place it in the middle. The player with the highest card value would take possession of the lowest card value. These were then placed at the bottom of that player's deck.

Now imagine what happens when players flip over a card with the same value, such as an ace. This marks the moment when you declare war. Both players would need to place three cards face down while saying, "I...De...clare...". Then, the fourth card is placed on top, card value showing, with each player saying, "War!" It's interesting because you are unsure whether your card value is higher, lower, or the same as your opponent's, yet you have the confidence of winning. This continues until one person has every single card.

The game can be entertaining and educational, depending on whom you're playing with. I learned three things from playing this card game with my oldest brother: (1) Patience. This game is so long, but when you are focused on beating your opponent, you do not mind waiting it out. (2) Persistence. There were times when I lost rounds, but I would end up winning the game. I would get mad, but would not quit. Even when it looked like I would lose, I still kept playing. (3) Perseverance. Sometimes I had what seemed like the worst combination of cards ever! My brother would trash talk me and try to discourage me, and I still kept believing that I could win. So I kept playing. That belief of prevailing and winning helped me to power through, whether I won the game or not.

The same is true for spiritual battles. Just like in the game, spiritual battles require patience, persistence, and unwavering perseverance. The difference between the two is that this spiritual walk is not a game. Our victory is already secured through Jesus Christ, who died on the cross for the remission of our sins, was buried, and resurrected. Your opponent, satan, will trash talk you, discredit you, and discourage you from believing that God, Jesus, and the Holy Spirit are real and that we are in a serious war. As I live and breathe, I assure you that this spiritual war is real and it is serious. I, for one, would like to know what I'm up against before going into fight mode.

The card game of I Declare War has a lot of unknowns, but in spiritual warfare, truths are revealed in how we should fight and which tools we should use. Oftentimes, we remain unaware of the power we possess as children of God. We read scriptures about how the power of life and death is in our tongue (Proverbs 18:21), but do we realize the true power that we possess? For this spiritual war, it is essential not only to know God but also to know yourself through His eyes and discern which weapons to use.

From the moment the title *I Declare War* came to me, I knew this book would center on spiritual warfare and the best way to fight back. I will share several personal experiences with warfare and how I learned to fight back spiritually. It is my hope that everyone who reads this book is not only blessed, but encouraged and empowered to take a stand against the enemy. Let us boldly fight back against the dark forces of this world. It is time to declare war!

Early Exposure

All My Life

While it may sound cliché to say I have been in church all my life, it rings true for me. I was one of those who regularly attended church programs. I went to Sunday School, Sunday service, Bible Study, Vacation Bible School, revivals, conferences, and special services like Healing and Deliverance nights. If there was a program happening at church, I was there.

The first church I remember attending was a Baptist Church in Little Rock, Arkansas. I have memories of arriving early to attend Sunday School for children and serving as a junior usher on Youth Sundays. My mom will never let me forget about my commitment to ushering, as she often shares a funny memory of that time. Supposedly, when asked if I was a Christian, my response was, "I'm not a Christian, I'm an usher!" Though I do not recall saying this, I have heard my mom retelling this moment several times, so I know it actually happened.

Needless to say, my dedication to God stemmed from early exposure to Him. Though I may not have understood everything in depth, my mom's consistent efforts to bring us to church shaped my perspective and fueled my desire for Him. This early exposure laid an invaluable, firm foundation in my life. It's how God became a focal point for me despite being exposed to things outside of church as well.

Looking back on these early experiences, I have come to understand the vital role that being a gatekeeper plays in our lives. A gatekeeper's job is to be watchful, to be on guard, to protect, and to filter out what does not belong. Being a gatekeeper over your eyes and ears does not require a lifetime church membership, being perfect, or being well-put together. What you need is a personal relationship with God and to be your genuine, authentic self. As you draw closer to Him, He will beautify and perfect your life by fine-tuning your sight and hearing to His own.

The devil, your adversary, will use different tactics and devices to entice you and your children. He uses avenues such as music, movies, television shows, social media, and more. Demonic and satanic messages are often hidden in what we listen to and watch, or allow our children to engage in. Be mindful of what you expose yourself or your children to, and what you teach them to accept—whether purposely or carelessly. Knowing that the devil uses such subtle tactics is enough to be spiritually guarded, for your sake and theirs. He doesn't even like you! Do not grant someone who doesn't like you access to your mind, body, heart, or soul.

If you read 1 Kings and 2 Kings, you will find that those who were tasked with being shepherds over Israel and Judah did not always obey God. Some of them were not good gatekeepers and led these nations into sinning against Him. This had dire consequences for those kings, their descendants, and the nations of Israel and Judah. There will also be dire consequences for those in the authoritative position of a gatekeeper who have since become lax or have fallen asleep. Do not be one of them.

Where is my Testimony?

Years later, when I was around the age of 11, my family and I migrated to a new church. This church was Nondenominational and located in North Little Rock, Arkansas. At the time, I did not know much about the Holy Spirit, but I could sense when the presence of God was in the building. It was a relatively small church, so children and teens stayed in the sanctuary with the adults. Even though I did not have a deep understanding of God, Jesus, and the Holy Spirit, I had a thirst for knowledge and was a quick learner. I brought a tablet to church with me so I could take notes on the sermons and learn more about God. The moments that truly caught my attention, though, were praise and worship and the sharing of testimonies.

The praise and worship portions of service would be on fire! So much so that angelic beings were seen during a Sunday service that my oldest brother recorded. I remember being in awe that one of the angelic beings appeared close to me in the video! To this day, though, we cannot see any of the angelic beings on the recording. I felt, and still feel, honored to have had them in our midst. They looked like bright translucent lights to me and reminded me of the movie *Angels in the Outfield.* Two of my favorite lines from that movie are "You got an angel with you right now" and "It could happen". I can tell you that it did indeed happen, and we did have angels in our midst that day.

Witnessing miracles, signs, and wonders like that made me want to get to know God even more. It was not at all scary to me, and I knew it was not magic. I soaked up every bit of knowledge that I could for an 11-year-old, but was confused during testimony time. I listened intently to the adults share how God had healed them or a family member, how money appeared in their mailbox, and more. I was happy for them, but confused as to why I didn't have a testimony to share. How could I have been in church for 11 years and not have a testimony?

So my eagerly naive self sat in Bible Study one evening, talking to God in my head. I asked God to give me a test so that I could have a testimony. What 11-year-old *asks* to be tested? The request was so innocent, but I was serious about it. Looking back and knowing what I know now, I would have kept my mouth shut! There are some tests that you do not want, did not ask for, and wish to return to sender. But here I was, 11 years old, asking God to give me a test so that I, too, may share a testimony.

Can you see now how being introduced to God and constantly exposed to Him and His presence was taking root in my heart and driving my decision-making? This is crucial because as parents and parental figures, we are instructed to "direct…children onto the right path, and when they are older, they will not leave it" (Proverbs 22:6). The way you teach or train your child is what they will remember, lean on, run to, and utilize when they are older. If you teach or train hate, that is what they will gravitate toward. If you teach or train love, that is what they will access and produce. You cannot make the choice for your child, but how and what you teach, train, and direct them on does matter. Teach and train wisely.

Tent Revival Salvation

Our church brought in a local prophet to host a tent revival during the summer of when I was 11. If you are unaware, Arkansas is down south and full of country folk. Although having a revival outside in a tent may have seemed country, I loved every bit of it. I remember people walking in off the street to get saved, healed, and delivered, and again seeing miracles take place. I was captivated!

I cannot recall how many nights the tent revival lasted, but I got saved close to the last night. I cannot remember the message that was spoken or the songs that were sung, but the people came with hunger in their hearts. I cannot tell you how many people were there or who was in attendance, but it was packed! What I do remember and what I can tell you is when the man of God made the appeal to be saved, my cousin grabbed my arm, pulling me to the altar with her.

I did not want to go up there. It was not as if he hadn't made the same appeal the previous nights of the revival. He did. It was not that I didn't love God or love being in His presence. I did. I did not want to go up there because I was really shy as a kid and did not like talking to strangers, being in front of a crowd, or being the focus of attention.

Yet, here I was standing side-by-side hand-in-hand with my cousin. By the time the man of God came toward us, I felt my breath quicken and a heaviness on my chest. I don't mean 'heaviness' as in pain and suffering. No, the air was thicker and it felt as if I was having an anxiety attack except I wasn't. I may not be doing justice with my description, but I want to make clear that the presence I felt was not scary, tormenting, terrifying, or painful. It was powerful and holy. It was the presence of the Lord.

So my cousin and I confessed our sins and were saved (Romans 10:9-10). As the man of God prayed and laid hands on my cousin, her grip loosened from my hand and I was standing there by myself. My eyes were closed, so I had no idea which direction she went. Then I felt the man of God stand in front of me, and he prayed and laid his hands on me. Immediately, I began to speak in tongues and fell to the ground. It was so strange to me. Nothing like that had ever happened to me or come out of my mouth before then. Without realizing what I was doing, I tried my best to stop the tongues from flowing and they did.

As I mentioned earlier, I did not have a deep understanding of God, Jesus, and the Holy Spirit at this age. If I did, I would not have tried to stop the tongues from flowing. My advice to my younger self for this moment would be: "Do not quench the Holy Spirit! Do not stop Him! Let Him flow freely and embrace Him!" When you know better you *should* do better. Once I understood what I did, I apologized to God and the Holy Spirit and repented of my ignorance. Thankfully, I have since learned to embrace the Holy Spirit more and more.

For anyone looking to learn more about the Holy Spirit, I recommend reading the Bible first, as all scripture is inspired by Him (2 Timothy 3:16-17). Most Bibles now have an index where you can go straight to that page to find more information about that topic, along with the corresponding scriptures. I recommend the entire Bible, as His footprints are evident all throughout the book. I would also recommend reading *Good Morning, Holy Spirit* by Benny Hinn or listening to the teachings of Kathryn Kuhlman.

You might be wondering why I included all of this information here. Do you not know what a huge blow you deliver to satan when you boldly declare that Jesus is Lord and you believe that God raised Him from the dead? You are declaring the Good News! No enemy is ecstatic when their opponent gains a level of access to heavy artillery, backup, power, knowledge, and so on. Likewise, the devil is not ecstatic when you take a step towards salvation. He does not want you to gain access to your spiritual backup, power, and heavy artillery. Instead, he wants to get and keep you distracted, confused, and oblivious. Oftentimes, we adopt an "I'll believe it when I see it" or "Because I didn't see it, it didn't happen" attitude. These are not the types of attitudes or mindsets needed for this kind of war.

> *For we are not fighting against flesh-and-blood enemies, but against evil rulers and authorities of the unseen world, against mighty powers in this dark world, and against evil spirits in the heavenly places. (Ephesians 6:12)*

This is the kind of war that we are fighting. You will not always "see it" with your physical eyesight, but it is happening all around you, day in and day out. And although the spiritual world can manifest in the natural world, if you fight this war naturally or humanly, <u>you</u> <u>will</u> <u>lose</u>! We are encouraged to "put on all of God's armor so that [we] will be able to stand firm against all strategies of the devil" (Ephesians 6:11). The enemy's strategies aren't pleasant or nice. They can be ruthless, unforgiving, relentless, painful, aggravating, heartless, and more. Even so, not one of his strategies are effective against the whole armor of God.

As you continue reading, I will highlight each piece of armor of God and provide examples of how I have used them in the past and how I am still using them today. While I will highlight them individually, they are the most effective when combined and utilized together.

BELT OF TRUTH

First Test

Let's fast-forward to the summer of 2007: I had been in church all my life, check! I had gotten saved, check! I had been baptized, check! I continued to take notes during sermons, check! And I was learning more and more about God, check!

I had increasingly come out of my shell, no longer afraid to stop people from walking during certain parts of the service or asking them to spit their gum out. That's right, I was still an usher! I did not realize it at the time, but ushering played a crucial role in teaching me to be sensitive to the Spirit, to be disciplined, and to be on guard. I also did not realize how much of a target I would become to the enemy simply because I had chosen to follow God. Looking back, I probably would have avoided one of my first tests if I understood how the enemy appears and operates.

I had experienced heartbreak at such a young age, which seemed devastating at the time. The enemy took advantage of that situation to make things worse for me, but God never took His hands off of my life. The heartbreak was not life-threatening, and everything still worked out for my good. I am grateful to have experienced it because I learned from it.

At the time, I was interested in a guy who happened to be related to a classmate of mine. Despite finding him attractive, I was unsure about dating him. Because of this uncertainty, I thought I could do like Abraham's servant did when he was looking for a wife for Isaac (Genesis 24:14). I figured if Abraham and his servant could do it, so could I. My faith in repeating what I read in the Bible was strong but misguided and misused. I said, "God, if he is the one, let him say this to me." I do not remember the exact phrase or words I used, but the guy spoke words that closely resembled what I said to God. I was stunned and giddy because I thought it worked! Little did I know, I had exposed myself to a potential spiritual attack because I was lusting with my eyes.

During that relationship, I did get upset with God because I felt like He misled me. Why would this guy say similar words to the ones I used in my request if God didn't send him? The more upset I got, the more I started thinking, "Maybe this stuff doesn't really work and maybe God doesn't really answer prayers and requests." I was referring to the direct communication God had with men like Abraham and Moses. I was expecting to hear from God like they did, and it didn't happen the way I thought it would. Thoughts of doubt about God's existence and power then crept into my mind, which is a deceptive tactic of the enemy. Any thought that causes you to doubt the existence of, power of, and knowledge of God is deceptive and needs to be taken captive. Immediately!

Consider, for a moment, the story of Pharaoh's magicians attempting to discount and discredit God's power by performing magic (Exodus 7). Each time Moses and Aaron performed a miracle by God's authority, Pharaoh's sorcerers performed magic by the authority of evil spirits (dark world). Pharaoh's officials did what they could, but they were still no match for God:

> *Pharaoh's magicians tried to do the same thing with their secret arts, but this time they failed. And the gnats covered everyone, people and animals alike. 'This is the finger of God!' the magicians exclaimed to Pharaoh. (Exodus 8:18-19a)*

Even these sorcerers or magicians had to acknowledge God while also acknowledging that their power was limited. Do not be deceived in thinking that the enemy—your enemy—does not know he has limited powers. He is limited where God is limitless. Those who have accepted Christ into their lives have access to an unlimited God.

I was upset with God, but it wasn't warranted. In fact, it was pretty foolish of me to get upset with Him (Proverbs 19:3). One, I was not Abraham nor his servant. I did not swear an oath to anyone, and no one swore an oath to me. Two, I was deceived into thinking my request being answered was from God. It wasn't. The request was made by the desire of my flesh, not according to God's will for me, which opened the door to me sinning against Him. Three, God didn't confirm that he was the guy. A lot of times we get mad at God or blame Him when something does not happen the way we want it to, or if He gives us what we asked for and it still does not turn out like we thought it would.

If you do not remember anything else written in this book, remember what I said earlier about being mindful of what you expose yourself to. I had exposed myself to sinning against God because the guy I liked was cute and I desired to be in a relationship with him. My spiritual guard was down, and the enemy was having a field day with my mind and my emotions. This is a prime example of what can happen when you are caught unaware.

I didn't like being on a mental and emotional roller coaster in that relationship or sinning against God. I was depressed, I isolated myself, and I went days without eating. I started hearing thoughts like, "It would be better if you weren't here so you don't have to deal with the pain". I even had a vision of me walking to the lake behind our house and thinking, "No one will miss me. They will be better off without me." I wasn't actively suicidal; just the ideation was there. I remember being confused as to why those thoughts came into my mind. I had heard the word "suicide" before and had watched shows and movies that referenced it, but never before had I had the thought that *I* should take my own life. I didn't even want to, so I knew that the thoughts weren't my own.

There was a serious internal conflict happening. It was one of the first moments I discovered just how strong a mind battle could be. At the time, I was not in a place of spiritual maturity where I could brace myself against these attacks. But God! He knew to place me among people who could and would pray for me. As they continuously prayed for me, I felt strengthened in my emotions and in my mind. The attacks ceased, and those thoughts were no longer looming over me.

While I was able to shake loose from these thoughts, I did not take them lightly. It is not always easy to break away from suicidal thoughts. Sometimes, you need to talk with a mental health professional. Remove any shame or embarrassment associated with getting help, whether from a church official or a therapist. Invest in yourself by getting the help you need, when and where you need it. Do not allow the enemy to torment you with thoughts and visions of death. If you do not know how to take those thoughts captive, connect with someone who can. When you're ready, you will do whatever is necessary to break free.

When I was ready to break free and get off that roller coaster, I started journaling to God. I wrote out how I felt, what I thought, what I needed, and anything else that I wanted to say or ask. I was not too confident in praying yet, so I thought I could write my prayers out and it would still be effective. It was!

I remember one journal entry in particular where I was crying and my tears stained the paper. I remember signing the bottom of the journal entry and writing, "Rescue me". We went to Bible Study that same night, and at the end of the service, the Pastor asked if anyone needed prayer. I went to the altar but I didn't say why I needed prayer. I just cried. I stood at the altar and cried. The Pastor hugged me and I felt comforted. Somehow, I ended up on the floor, eyes still closed and tears still falling. I clearly heard the Pastor say something I will never forget. He said, "God said He is coming to rescue you and He won't delay." I cried even more, but this time out of relief and happiness. That was confirmation that God heard me, saw what I wrote, and was coming for me.

The Lord hears his people when they call to him for help. He rescues them from all their troubles. The Lord is close to the brokenhearted; he rescues those whose spirits are crushed. The righteous person faces many troubles, but the Lord comes to the rescue each time. (Psalms 34:17-19)

I was in trouble, I was broken, and my spirit was crushed. But the Lord is faithful in keeping His promises! He did not delay in rescuing me. This was not the only time that He rescued me, but it was the first time I realized that He could and would do it.

Some might wonder, "What's the difference between the first request and the second? Didn't satan hear the second request, too?" All I can say is with the second request—the plea for rescue—I received confirmation and an assurance. When God says He will do something, He will do it! No devil in hell will be able to stop Him! Plus, no enemy will rescue their opponent or help them out.

This experience deepened my understanding of God's nature and character, what it is and what it is not. It helped me see the enemy's character and his deceptive tactics. It also taught me how to be honest with God about how I saw myself versus how He saw me. Even today, I am still learning and being reminded of God's character, and He is revealing more about how He sees me.

The Belt of Truth is the foundation for the whole armor of God. More than that, it involves acknowledging God and understanding His character, being honest with God about your missteps and disappointments, recognizing your identity in Him, and embracing the freedom only He can provide. Where there is truth, there you will also find freedom (John 8:32).

Even after this test, I stumbled many times. Though I read my Bible earnestly, I was getting first-hand spiritual knowledge and training. Through my stumbling and restoration, I experienced God in a way that just reading about doesn't do any justice. God's grace and restoration, in the midst of these early challenges, unveiled His character while highlighting the deceptive tactics of the enemy. God doesn't desire for you to be completely unaware, blind, or ignorant of what's going on. He will reveal the truth to you; you just have to be open to see it and to receive it.

Prayer

Father, thank You for the Belt of Truth. Thank You for sharing Your character with me so I can get to know You better. Thank You for revealing the enemy's character so I know what to watch out for. Thank You for allowing me to be honest about where I am in life, how I view myself, or how I view my situations. Spirit of Truth, do not depart from me. Teach me more about God and myself. Help me to walk in the freedom provided by the sacrificial blood of Jesus Christ. In Jesus' name, I pray. Amen.

Breastplate of Righteousness

Love TKO

Being rescued by God felt like sunshine on a cloudy day, fresh strawberry cupcakes, minty-fresh breath, homemade vanilla ice cream, and warm bear hugs. When that relationship ended and the spiritual ties to that roller coaster were severed, I felt as free as a dog taken off of its leash, able to roam without restrictions. It no longer held power over me.

The depression no longer held power over me. The back-and-forth with the guy no longer held power over me. Those negative, deceptive thoughts no longer held power over me. The enemy had to resort to a different tactic to get me off course. I have to admit, though, that I did not see it coming until afterward because I had gotten comfortable.

I had been dating a guy for almost a year when we started to have major problems. *Another relationship, I know.* We eventually broke up but remained in communication with each other. I was under the impression that we would reconcile, but I was mistaken. I started receiving reports of him with a girl I knew, and who had previously made attempts to "befriend" me. I recall how she would invite me to different religious group events and outings, and had even offered to do my hair.

As a Black woman, no one touches my hair unless I trust you to do so. At the time, I did trust that her intentions toward me were pure. However, I was so consumed with being a "new" me and embracing new experiences that I could not tell the difference between friendly interactions and scouting behaviors. I got wise, though, when one day she approached me at the end of Bible Study and asked questions about my relationship with the guy. I remember the conversation vividly, especially what she said at the end:

"Are you and [so-and-so] dating?" She asked me.

"Yeah." I answered.

"Why you ain't tell me y'all was dating?" She inquired.

I looked at her puzzled because it was no one's business whether or not we were dating. Until we made it publicly known, our business was our business. I just smiled and said, "We just started dating. A lot of people thought we were dating before and we weren't. We literally just started dating."

She then tells me, "Oh. Girl, you've got a good man. I mean, he loves God, he's from a good family, he's smart…you better hold on to him or I will."

Her "joke" about holding onto him was very telling of how she meant to invade my inner circle. Why say that if we are friends? I did not dismiss it as a joke, and neither did my real friend who also heard her say it. We were both shocked by the statement and confused as to why it was mentioned in the first place. Neither of us could have imagined saying such a thing to a person we were truly friends with. I later realized that the girl had been scouting for information and weak spots in my relationship. She found them, too.

There are some conflicting perspectives about what happened from the people involved. She has her perspective, he has his own, and I have mine. Despite these conflicting perspectives, when the two of them began talking or dating, I got three initial reports from people in three different friend circles. I knew the information they shared was credible, and I was furious! Some might say, "Well, you two were broken up so there was no reason for you to be mad." Normally, I would agree, but not in this case. He and I were still communicating to a degree that reflected rekindling the relationship, and the girl had made attempts in the past to "befriend" me. I absolutely had a right to be upset. Talk about a Love TKO!

My mom says I have this look that I get sometimes. She says it communicates, "I'm serious and someone's about to get hurt." I usually deny having such facial expressions, but I could not deny it in this instance. If I could have set them on fire with my eyes, I would have stood there and watched them both burn. I could not even process the situation because my anger was burning hotter than the furnace in hell!

It wasn't that my emotions were not valid; they were. It was okay for me to feel betrayed, hurt, and upset. What was not okay was that my emotions were growing too intense and I had allowed them to start making decisions for me. I could feel my emotions grow calloused and my hatred grow stronger. I did not hear God's voice as often and I stopped seeking Him. I had decided that my life would be my own and that I would do what everybody else was doing because at least they weren't hurting.

Oh, how blind and wrong I was! I didn't see, at the time, the wedge being drawn between me and God. It was not that God didn't reach out to me; He did. It was that my emotions clouded my judgment, rationale, and any spiritual connection I had with God. Every inch of distance between me and God was an opportunity for satan to get in between and make the distance bigger. But how loving and caring is our God!

I started getting sick, like physically sick. I would get headaches and stomachaches, feel nauseous, and more. While that doesn't seem very caring, it was. By getting sick, I was driven to seek God for help. I just remember hearing Him say, "Let it go." Three simple words and I was struggling to follow the instructions. *How do I let it go? Do you not know what they did? Do you not see how that hurt me?* I basically threw a tantrum, trying to get God to understand how much I was affected by the situation. He did see it. He saw all of it and yet He was asking me to trust Him. God showed me that my sickness was linked to me harboring those emotions. For Him to be able to help me, I had to let go.

Let's pause here and acknowledge this crucial truth about God: He cares deeply for you. He does care about your emotions and how you feel; however, He is not an emotionally driven God. There are plenty of examples in the Bible where God could have wiped people out in His anger, yet He exercised great patience and love. While God is concerned about you and what affects you, expecting Him to move solely based on how you feel is misguided. God will not be your ride-or-die in the backseat as you try to exact revenge. It doesn't work like that. "Whoever is slow to anger has great understanding, but he who has a hasty temper exalts folly" (Proverbs 14:29 ESV). How much more true is this of God who is slow to anger and filled with unfailing love (Numbers 14:18; Exodus 34:6-7)?

Emotions, if left unchecked, can get us into trouble. Do not discount your emotions; be aware of how you're feeling so you can have better control over them. Controlling your emotions is a sign of wisdom (Proverbs 15:18). I was losing control because my emotions were so intense and I didn't know how to handle them. The enemy seized his opportunity like a scavenging hyena, but the Lord didn't give up on me. He let me know that He was still there, willing to love me and help me. He only asked that I do something on my end: Let it go. I fought against it but my desire to be healthy again outweighed my hurt and rage. I gave up fighting and decided to let it go so that I could be free once again. I had to be honest with God about what happened and how it impacted me. I had to confront and release the emotions trapped within me. I had to work to forgive them both, whether they apologized or not.

Was it easy? No! I won't lie and say it was. My journey toward forgiveness was a gradual progression rather than an instant one. I did not realize until much later that by letting go, I was performing more than just an action. I was choosing to embrace healing, have a renewed sense of self, and to be obedient to His commands.

Emotional Detox

Three things that really helped me were talking to God, journaling, and being amongst true friends. I was honest enough with God to tell Him how much it hurt and how I needed Him to heal me. I would then journal what I felt like I could not say with words. I also had a friend group that made sure I did not get complacent with the emotions I felt. They continuously checked on me, shared positive words with me, made me laugh, and forced me to get out (whether I wanted to or not).

The more I talked to God, journaled, and spent time with true friends, the more I felt like myself and not some anger-possessed maniac. I found myself breathing better and smiling more. I was healing! Even though it was not an overnight completion, I was still grateful for the changes I noticed. I even wrote about it for a creative writing assignment:

> *Hate is a powerful drug, but love is stronger. Love will cause you to rise above yourself and forgive those who have hurt you, even if they don't ask to be forgiven. Sometimes, it just means being the bigger person. In the end, I won. (Vanley, Bree. 2012. "Emotional Detox". Unpublished paper.)*

At the time, I did not realize that one of my classmates was close to the girl. I also did not care. "Emotional Detox" was never meant to focus on the two people who had caused the hurt. It was intended to show my journey from harboring ill feelings to accepting healing. I learned a good lesson in a very painful way: "Guard your heart above all else, for it determines the course of your life" (Proverbs 4:23). I was heading down a dangerous road by allowing my emotions to get the best of me. I was stirring hate in my heart and spewing it from my mouth, a clear sign that I was living in darkness (1 John 2:9-11) and was becoming a fool (Proverbs 10:18). That has never been, nor will it ever be, God's desire for my life or yours.

I want to interject here to say that it is okay to acknowledge that you were hurt. It is also okay to acknowledge who hurt you. You need to acknowledge it so you can work to be released from it. It is not God's desire that you hold grudges or hold on to hurt, bitterness, rage, etc. In fact, He compels us to get rid of it (Ephesians 4:31) and to forgive (v. 32). Sometimes it is difficult to let go and forgive because, in an odd way, the pain, hurt, bitterness, and rage are comforting. It's what fuels you! It is also another deception tool used by the enemy to keep you bound, stuck, and trapped.

Imagine driving off the car lot in a brand-new, never-before-driven Jaguar XJ. You enjoy it all week, driving wherever you please before needing to fill it up with gas. If you put regular fuel in your tank, you have just now put your engine at risk for malfunction and underperformance. If you use the premium fuel, however, your Jag will continue to run smoothly. The premium fuel will ensure that your vehicle has what it needs to function properly.

Much like fueling up a vehicle improperly, if you fuel up on hatred, bitterness, and rage, you set yourself up for malfunction and deterioration. If you fuel up on the fruit of the Spirit (Galatians 5:22-23), you set yourself up to be free from the desires of your sinful nature (v. 19-21). The type of fuel you choose will greatly impact the quality and duration of your life. Choose carefully.

I received firsthand knowledge of what it's like to fill up on an improper fuel type. Trusting God when He told me to let it go not only revealed His love and care for me in a new light, but it also released me from those negative thoughts and emotions. I was no longer trapped by bitterness, rage, and hatred. I was free.

Whose Servant are you Anyway?

My relationships have taught me a lot about God and myself. I remember telling my mom one day that our relationship with others is a mirror extension of our relationship with God. What I meant was the actions you take to nourish and cultivate your relationship with God will, in turn, help you to nourish and cultivate your relationship with others. Do not expect any relationship to thrive—even if it appears promising—if you place God in any position but first. I, once again, learned this painfully but am grateful for the lesson learned.

The last relationship I was in was very short-lived. It was over by the second month, but somehow we had stretched it to six months. And I do mean stretch! I was not looking to date anybody at the time, however, he snuck up on me. I did something nice for him one day, as is in my nature to do, and he took notice of me. I thought, "What's the harm in just talking to him?" So we did. We talked for a few weeks and realized there was interest on both sides, so we started to date. Our interests grew quickly, and we were enamored with each other. At least I was. Honestly it was more of a euphoric experience, from which a soul tie was formed.

One day as I was driving to work with my radio off, I suddenly heard a voice from my passenger seat say, "He's a decoy," all calm and matter-of-fact. I looked over to my passenger's seat, knowing that I was the only person in the car. I could feel the presence of someone, but could not see them. Then I started talking out loud,

"He's a decoy? How? No he's not. He loves God and he knows the Bible. There's no way he could be a decoy." As I continued to dismiss the statement, I could feel the presence leave my vehicle. However, those words stayed with me: "He's a decoy".

I wrestled with that statement for a few days. *How could he be a decoy? Surely, I would have seen that coming, right?* Wrong. A few days passed, and I drove to work in silence again. I heard the same voice, except it was more solid and firm. "He's a decoy." I knew it was the Holy Spirit talking to me, and this time I burst into tears. I was talking to God and crying and driving all at the same time. I finally said, "What do You want me to do? Do you want me to give him up? Because I will. I love him but I love You more. I'll give him up for You. If You say he's a decoy, then he's a decoy and I will let him go. It will hurt me, but I will let him go. I want what You want for me and who You want for me. Your will trumps mine."

This is humility and surrender at its finest—to give up one's own desires for God's. Not everyone can say things like this to God and mean it. It was not any less painful to do so, but absolutely worth it. I have not regretted it a day since.

God started showing me that I placed more emphasis on my relationship with the guy rather than my relationship with Him. I had taken on values which were important to the guy but contradictory to God (Matthew 6:24; Amos 3:3). In short, I had tipped over into idol worship without even being aware of it. I knew for God to reveal this information to me that it was important to Him and He was giving me a choice: Him or the guy. God was not giving me an ultimatum; He was actually testing me to see what was in my heart. I tell God that I love Him all the time, but would I choose Him over my wants, wishes, and desires when given the choice? This was a great test that I almost failed.

It is easy to choose God when it's just you and Him. When you have family, friends, or a significant other, you have to be diligent not to elevate them to God's position. He does not share. This is not a dig at anyone who has had a moment of choosing something or someone over God. I am just exposing how easy it is to be tempted to do so. Sometimes we choose watching TV over studying our Bible or praying. Sometimes we look for answers from things and people before we seek answers from God. No one is exempt from being tested in this area, but not everyone is successful in passing.

One of the greatest commandments is to "love the Lord your God with all your heart, all your soul, and all your strength" (Deuteronomy 6:5). Jesus later added, "...and all your mind" (Matthew 22:37). Loving God and putting Him first has always been the greatest commandment for those who are His children because everything starts and ends with Him. He is Sovereign and He does not play about His position. He will not fight you on it or force you to put Him first, but His stance does not change. Failure to give God His rightful place yields disastrous results.

Even the Israelites, God's chosen people, underwent periods of forsaking God by worshiping idols and following the religious practices of the surrounding nations. They did not keep God first or follow His commands. This led to them being defeated in some battles, having evil rulers, and even losing portions of their land. You can accept or reject the Lord, but if you reject Him, you make yourself out to be an enemy of God. I do not know about you, but God is the one being I do not want as an enemy!

Although I have included examples of my relationship mishaps, I have no ill feelings toward any of my exes. I have forgiven them and have prayed for them on multiple occasions, whether we have stayed in communication or not. I only mention these stories about my relationships because they highlight the significance of the Breastplate of Righteousness. The Breastplate of Righteousness is focused on obeying God's commands, living honorably, and protecting our hearts against sin.

I had moments of triumph and moments of failure when it came to this. There were times when I would fully obey God's commands and live honorably, which protected my heart from sin. There were other times when I did what was pleasing to my flesh. When this would happen, God corrected me much like a parent would do. He reminded me that we are commanded to love Him and to love others (Matthew 22:39), to be holy because He is holy (1 Peter 1:15-16), and to guard our hearts (Proverbs 4:23). These are not unsolicited suggestions; they are keys to help you live a life that is pleasing to the Lord.

Once I realized that by not obeying these commands that I became an easy target for the devil, I repented and purposed to start practicing them. I am not perfect at it and do not always get it right, but I do put these commands into practice. I have learned how to protect my heart using God's wisdom, knowledge, and understanding. I encourage you to work on forgiving others, loving them, and guarding your heart. Put these commands into practice and keep practicing them, even if you do not get them right the first time. The benefits of doing so will far outweigh the temporary pain, hurt, and suffering you experience (Romans 8:18).

Prayer

Lord, help me to release the emotions and grudges I have held against those who hurt me. Help me to forgive them as You forgive me. Help me to release them and the situation into Your hands so I don't malfunction or deteriorate. God, break every soul tie in my life! Send Your Holy Ghost fire to sever the connections and to burn up any remains. Free me in the name of Jesus! Holy Spirit, help me to live more honorably, to obey God's commands, and to better guard my heart. Strengthen me so that I may better practice loving others and forgiving them. In Jesus' name, I pray. Amen.

Shield of Faith

Wind Knocked Out

By this time, I had a deeper understanding of the Lord's nature and character: loving, patient, forgiving, kind, gentle, and self-controlled (Galatians 5:22-23). The frequent testing I endured provided personal opportunities for me to witness His patience, kindness, forgiveness, and love. I was not without sin, but I had learned the importance of being honest with God, seeking forgiveness, and repenting. I recall a time when I was preparing to pray to God and ask for forgiveness after sinning. I heard a voice in my head say, "Why are you asking God to forgive you? Do you think he will forgive you after what you did, especially since you said you wouldn't do it again? Surely God will not forgive you." I believed it, too. I delayed asking God for forgiveness because I thought I was not worthy or deserving of His forgiveness.

And it was a bold-faced, bald-headed lie!

God then started sending me messages on repentance. I heard the same repentance appeal in three different sermons. I quickly realized that God was reaching out to me. God loves unconditionally and He graciously forgives us when our hearts are truly repentant. God calls and compels us to repent through His voice, messengers, dreams, visions, and so on. To know God is to know His voice, and I knew He was calling me to repent. So I did. Then I challenged that thought that told me, "You are disqualified and unworthy." God has deemed me as qualified and worthy, just as He has deemed you. Do not be deceived in thinking otherwise.

As I gained a deeper understanding of God's character, I was also learning the enemy's character: a liar, deceiver, tempter, and murderer. He is a thief who comes to steal, kill, and destroy (John 10:10) and is essentially any and everything contrary to God. As the prince of this world (John 12:31; John 14:30), he often tempts us through the lust of the flesh, the lust of the eyes, and the pride of life (1 John 2:15-16). Jesus faced similar temptations yet provided the perfect example for how we should respond (Matthew 4:1-11). Rebuking the devil requires more than simply believing that God exists. We have to know God's voice and character, who we are in God, and what we possess. This happens by spending time with God much like you would your friends, family, or significant other.

As I discovered more about myself in God, I was reminded that I am indeed a fighter. My oldest brother and I often laugh and joke about our childhood misbehaviors. We each blame the other for being troublesome while attempting to declare our innocence. He does not hesitate to bring up several incidents, including the time when I jumped into one of his fights. He did not need my help at all. He packed a powerful punch, and his giant height gave him a great advantage. I jumped in the middle of one of his fights because there was no way someone would fight my brother while I just watched. It didn't matter that my brother's opponent was another male. What mattered to me was defending a loved one.

I could see my brother and this guy squaring up, and I ran from where I was and stood next to my brother. I don't recall if he immediately realized I was standing next to him, if he tried to send me back to the house, or what. What I do remember is, without warning, I did a few side-to-side hops and double-punched this guy in the stomach. I was trying to knock the wind out of him. For a young girl, I was heavy-handed, so I knew the punch hurt. Needless to say, the fighting between those two stopped, and my brother and I went home.

You would think I would be cautious to intervene between two teen males fighting. You would think I would hesitate to punch a guy, as there is always a chance that he may hit back. However, there was no fear in me and I ran towards the fight with the faith and determination of overpowering the opponent by any means necessary. Likewise, when you are fighting back against the enemy, there is a boldness and determination needed for battle. Nervousness and fear will lead to your defeat; faith will lead to your victory. While I did not hesitate to fight the opponent—any opposition toward my brother was opposition toward me—I was using physical tactics, which would only get me so far. I did not realize until much later that there was a difference between fighting physically and fighting spiritually.

Officially Declaring War

Around the time of 2018, I had become more comfortable with praying to God out loud. Someone told me that I was an intercessor, but I hadn't had much experience interceding for others in prayer at this point. At least, not until trouble hit my family. If something or someone harasses, bothers, or threatens them, I have no problem fighting on their behalf. That is the very definition of an intercessor! You stand in the gap and fight on behalf of someone else.

I recall worry hitting my heart like cement bricks being thrown at me. I was frantic, not knowing what to do to help my family or myself. Uncertain of where to go, I knew to go somewhere where I felt the presence and power of God. I drove to the church I attended at the time and parked out front. There were no services scheduled and no other vehicle was present. I parked and prayed. I cried and prayed. Then, I prayed some more. I was not praying for myself, though; I was interceding on behalf of my family. I was not completely sure if I was interceding correctly, but I had faith that God heard me and would respond.

When I finished praying, I sat in silence for a little bit. I asked God for a sign, something to show me that He heard me and would respond. I turned my car back on and prepared to drive home, but stopped as "Mention" by Fresh Start Worship began to play on the radio. Initially, the lyrics did not seem to fit what I put before God. But I listened to the words and I heard God say, "This is your sign." The revelation was this: Call on the name of Jesus! Whatever tries to put you in a state of distress, torment, fear, worry, etc. has nothing on the name of Jesus! Every single thing has to bow at His name! To sum it up, God was telling me to trust that He had the situation under control. I immediately thanked Him, praising and honoring Him for the swift response.

In the following months, I saw God move on behalf of myself and my family. He was providing, blessing, and protecting as I had never experienced before. I was amazed and grateful! I had even called that year my "Ram in the Bush Year" because I witnessed the Lord moving in supernatural ways. During moments of discouragement, God would remind me of this song or I would hear it at what seemed like perfectly random moments. My hope and strength were then restored, and I continued to intercede and thank God for hearing me and moving on behalf of my plea. Prayer and intercession work! Do not give up praying and interceding for your family, yourself, others, or this world. Your prayer is powerful and effective (James 5:16).

After realizing that intercession made a difference, something arose on the inside of me. It was not quite revenge, but a no-nonsense approach towards the devil. I remember telling him that he messed up in targeting my family and that it would have been better to simply target me. There was a spiritual fervor inside me that I had not noticed before. I remember walking around my living room, calling the devil out, and talking bad to him. I told him that I was coming for him and I meant it! I could no longer sit idly on the sidelines and watch others get spiritually attacked without intervening. No, I would go to God on their behalf and pray in their stead. I told the devil, "This means war!"

Praying is a command (1 Thessalonians 5:17), not a suggestion. It is one of the most powerful tools that a believer can use. Even if you are not sure how to pray, start small and build from there. Jesus gave us clear instructions for how to pray (Matthew 6:5-15; Luke 11:1-13), so there should be no excuse. You can also connect with others who can educate you and support you in this area. While each person should have an individual prayer life, it is also a good idea to pray with your family, friends, and church. I have seen great things happen when even two or three people are praying together (Matthew 18:19).

I have not always been confident in praying, and the enemy has tried to intimidate me so that I do not even try. But it is just that: intimidation. When I was asked to lead prayer at my church one night, the enemy attacked my body. I started feeling sick in my stomach and heard a voice tell me to call and ask for someone else to take my place. I almost did it, too, but I went anyway. I didn't feel the best, but I went anyway. I was nervous, but I prayed anyway. Do you know what happened next? The Holy Spirit took over my prayer! I was praying in tongues and snatching things back in the Spirit—the very thing the enemy was trying to prevent me from accomplishing. Do not allow him to intimidate you or distract you from what you have been commanded to do: to never stop praying.

Consistent prayer and intercession do not come without retaliation from the devil. The enemy retaliated against me because I flipped the script and declared war on him. He has tried to intimidate me with the presence of shadows or darkness at moments when I pray. Occasionally, I would feel physically sick when preparing to do Kingdom work. He has also tried to kill me more than once (which I will detail in a later chapter). Sometimes, the intimidation worked; other times, it drove me to pray more fervently.

I am saying all of this so that you do not go into war blindly or with misperceptions. The enemy's time on earth is limited (Revelations 12:12), and he will do whatever he can to steal, kill, and destroy you. But do not be intimidated or afraid. You have power and authority over him and his little minions.

Throwing in the Towel

While facing ongoing spiritual battles, I lost both of my grandmothers two weeks apart. It was devastating to lose part of my history, connection, and heritage. I soon became aware that I had no remaining grandparents, as both had been preceded in death by their husbands. Grief began to set in, especially after believing God would heal my maternal grandmother. I petitioned Him to heal her and to keep her alive just a little longer, but it did not happen. In reality, God can and will heal. However, He respects our desires and refrains from forcing us. My maternal grandmother was ready to go—a truth I did not accept until months after her death.

I could not blame her, either. Given the choice, who would willingly stay on earth to endure evil, turmoil, strife, low pay, and unbearable taxes? I would not personally choose this over going to a place where there is no hunger, no thirst, no pain, and no more tears (Revelations 7: 15-17). At the time, though, I struggled to understand why my prayers were not being answered

The sadness grew, and it became overwhelming. I did not want to participate in this war anymore. I no longer wanted to be considered a soldier in the army of the Lord, let alone be a recipient of His blessings. I recall telling God, "I can't deny who You are and what I've seen You do, but I'm okay with You not doing anything else for me. I'm good. You can bless other people, and I'm okay with that, but please don't bother with me." I smiled but wasn't happy. I laughed but I was masking my cries. I talked to people but I was not mentally present. In all actuality, I was done with life.

I was not suicidal, but I was done trying and putting forth effort. Nothing mattered to me at that point. I made up my mind that I was done with the things of God but still wanted to live. Crazy, right? I did not comprehend that wanting to live but dismissing the things of God was a contradiction. What is life without God? Without Him we exist and then die; with Him we die and yet live (John 3:36; 1 John 5:13; 1 Timothy 6:12).

I was having a serious mental battle during this period of grieving. It was similar to a tug-of-war battle. I lost enjoyment in several areas of my life, I was numb, and I was intent on throwing in the towel. But God wouldn't let me go so easily. While traveling to my paternal grandmother's funeral in Phoenix, Arizona, God spoke to me about throwing in the towel. This is what I wrote down once we landed:

As our plane reached 10,000 feet in the air, I noticed that I could no longer see cars, streets, or the landscape beneath me. All I could see below the plane was a sea of white clouds, floating and secure. I then looked out my window to see what was above us, and I could see just enough to tell that there was a layer of white clouds. The captain gets over the intercom to announce that we will be experiencing some turbulence on this flight. And here's the revelation: When you are experiencing turbulence of any kind in your life, be still, remain calm, and trust that He's got your back. I was reminded of this while flying to Phoenix. I could not see what was below me and could barely see what was in the sky. God will sometimes allow turbulence to hit our lives to shake us up a bit and get us back on track. God just wants you to know that He'll never stop loving and carefully caring for you. You are a jewel; a gem. So much value has been placed on the inside of you. Don't allow the turbulence to distract you and make you think that God can't turn it around. (Vanley, Bree. 2017. "Revelation from God". Unpublished paper.)

At a time when I felt dejected, lost, and hopeless, God still reached out to me. I will always honor and cherish this moment because of how God pursued me. I had thrown in the towel, yet He still pursued me. He still loved me. He still cared. I needed to hear those words He spoke to me. The words were "like honey—sweet to the soul and healthy for the body" (Proverbs 16:24). If you have ever experienced similar thoughts and emotions, then let this revelation ring true for you also. God loves you and cares for you. You are a jewel. And you are valuable to Him. God can and will turn things around.

Yes, I was sad. I was depressed, I was grieving, and I was trying to give up on God. But I never denied His existence nor His power, which is what the enemy wanted me to do because I was hurting so much. It was kind of like how Job's wife antagonized him to "curse God and die" (Job 2:9). I could not do it. As bad as I was hurting, the Spirit of Truth was still very much alive on the inside of me.

As you learn the very nature, character, and essence of God, guarding your heart becomes essential for continuing your walk with Christ. There is no way I would be permitted everlasting life had I blasphemed against the Holy Spirit. Denying His existence and power—especially after witnessing miracles, signs, and wonders—would have been a complete slap in the face! Be careful that your thoughts and emotions do not lead you to say or do things to blaspheme against the Holy Spirit. That sin will never be forgiven, no matter how much you repent (Matthew 12:31-32).

During this time in my life, I faced challenges that were difficult and, at moments, unbearable. My faith was tested in ways I had never before experienced. I threw the towel in and tried to give up on God, but He would not give up on me. He was so patient and understanding of what I was dealing with and what I was going through. God would speak to me in messages, revelations, and signs not only to remind me of who He is but who I am as well. Seeing God pursue and fight for me encouraged me to pursue and fight for Him (1 Timothy 6:12).

Whether or not you declare war on the enemy, prepare for the testing of your faith. Taking up the shield of faith ensures you stand firm in your beliefs and adopt a defensive stance against every fiery dart from the enemy. I had faith that God would see and hear my intercession for my family. In addition to that, my faith in God's character and nature kept me from blaspheming against His Spirit. In truth, I did not comprehend everything that was happening spiritually. Faith, however, requires that you look past what you cannot see and what you may not always understand (Hebrews 11:1). Taking up, putting on, and utilizing your shield of faith ensures that you root yourself evermore in God, while bracing the impact of the enemy's attack against you.

Prayer

Father, forgive me for moments when I have been discouraged in my faith and doubted You. Strengthen my mind and redirect my focus back to You instead of what it looks like. Holy Spirit, teach me to trust God more, even if I can't see how He's working or if I don't understand 100%. Lord, strengthen me so I may stand more firmly against the fiery darts targeting me or my family. I rebuke every weapon, dart, trick, or trap the enemy has formed against me. It shall not work! I proclaim freedom in my mind, my life, my family, my business, my workplace, my relationships, and my church. In Jesus' name, I pray. Amen.

HELMET OF SALVATION

God is Still God

The Shield of Faith and Helmet of Salvation are like conjoined twins to me. You do not have one without the other, as both deal with the mind. Granted, we need the full armor of God, but the Shield of Faith and Helmet of Salvation are intricately connected. To activate faith, my beliefs—the rooted thoughts in my mind—should be in line with unwavering assuredness. When we were kids, my oldest brother tried to convince me that I was adopted. I began asking questions because I was unsure if he was telling the truth. Although he was playing, it planted doubt in my mind, and I wavered in my assuredness. Contrary to that, no one can convince me that my name is anything other than Bree. I am sure, with no doubt in my mind, that my name is Bree. Not Brielle. Not Brittany. Not Breneka. Not Breanna. Just Bree. I am also unwaveringly sure that God loves me!

Let me take you back to 2017 when Trump was officially declared the President of the United States. I remember listening to the radio on my way to work that morning and hearing that announcement. Immediately, I was upset and had so many questions and concerns. *What does this mean for America? For Black America? What is the world going to look like? How did he win? Do people really want us to go backward?* So many thoughts entered my mind, and I began speaking them out loud to God. I was so upset that I stopped by Starbucks to get coffee. I was not an avid coffee drinker, so for me to stop and order some meant that I was distraught.

I was in line talking to God, allowing worry to fill my mind and heart. I was searching for answers on what would happen next and what this meant for our nation. It didn't make sense to me, but I desperately needed to hear what God had to say about the matter. As I prepared to pay for my order, I sat in silence. I wanted to hear twice as much as I had been speaking. When I rolled my window down to pay for my order, the worker greeted me and said, "The lady before you paid for your order." I pulled off, parked, and immediately praised and thanked God. I asked Him to bless that lady, who just happened to be Caucasian, for her kindness toward me. Then I heard Him say, "I am still God." He assured me not to worry and let me know He was still in control. My faith greatly increased that day, and I no longer worried about the future. I had to trust that God is still God. He has always been in control.

I did not turn a blind eye either. I was not ignorant of the fact that racist and prejudiced beliefs, attitudes, and actions resurfaced. Some came from classmates, co-workers, or strangers in passing. It was heartbreaking to witness, and I was personally disgusted by it. I did not say anything, though. God told me not to focus on that and to look past what I saw. So I did. One day, while waiting for my to-go order at Olive Garden, a middle-aged Caucasian woman sat next to me, and we began talking. She was so sweet, and I could feel the presence of God as we talked. She complimented my smile and shared this with me: "If more people could learn to be kind to each other and smile and treat people the way Jesus told us to treat people, this world would be so different. It doesn't matter if I'm white and you're black. We both love God, and God loves us."

She was right, too! The division that is of God is equal to separateness, meaning it cannot be mixed or intertwined with just anything. The division that comes from the devil is equal to jealousy, hatred, discrimination, racism, evilness, and annihilation. The two are different! You cannot be of God yet practice or execute devilish division. They do not mix. You will be considered a hypocrite (Mark 7:6; Matthew 7:4-5; Matthew 15:7-9) and lukewarm (Revelations 3:15-16), neither of which have a place in God.

As much as other people's speech and behavior made me want to develop deep-rooted negative thoughts about them, God kept showing me that I needed to soften my heart and see the world and people how He sees them (1 Samuel 16:7). God was calling me to walk in peace (Matthew 5:9) and to look deeper at what was happening spiritually. There was no need for me to be at war with my white brothers and sisters. That is what the enemy wants anyway. If he can get us to war within ourselves and against others, we are doing his work for him. The Philistines had the same idea when Israel and Judah, God's chosen people, had a civil war with each other. Why make it easier for the devil to divide and conquer? But do not get it twisted! God never has and never will condone anything sinful, wicked, or evil. Those who practice those things will get what they deserve (Romans 2:8-9).

Unqualified to Supervise

I used to think wickedness was only for the world. That was before some people (who also went to church) lied about my character, talked about me, and treated me with contempt. Such individuals create confusion because they profess one thing but display something different. They are hypocritical—like hot, melted butter that has started to solidify. Imagine spreading such butter on a plate of shrimp scampi. It will not look the same, feel the same, or taste the same. Neither does having an outward display of honoring God with your mouth when your heart is far from Him (Matthew 15:8).

It would be easy for me to say that there is no difference between Christians and the world. It would not be true, though. Those that belong to God have an unadulterated relationship with Him. They embody the true character of Christ, which is evident in their lives. They produce good fruit from being connected to the true vine (Jesus).

So now we can tell who are children of God and who are children of the devil. Anyone who does not live righteously and does not love other believers does not belong to God. (1 John 3:10)

I realized that not everyone who attends church has a personal relationship with God. Some people only have a personal relationship with the members and the pews. I was wise enough not to allow a handful of people to ruin my belief, perception, and access to God. If you claim to be of Christ and He is not evident in your life, I will question who you belong to. Such was the case with a previous supervisor of mine.

Since entering the workforce full-time in 2014, I have worked for some supervisors who were rude, manipulative, and, quite frankly, unqualified to be in a leadership position. I have had my name lied on, my pay lowered, my character and work ethic questioned, and fired from positions where supervisors allowed their emotions to get the best of them. In each scenario, the businesses either took significant losses, closed, or the supervisor was removed from their position. It wasn't just that God did not play about me. He doesn't, but there was more to it than that. At each of these locations where I worked, I represented God. I represented Him in how I worked and how I treated others.

So when these supervisors mishandled and mistreated me, they were doing that to God. And He responded.

During my last full-time position, I encountered the absolute worst supervisor I have ever had. I had been working there for about a year before she came. I was praying before, during, and after work because the environment seemed to be a cesspool for demonic activity. Because of my constant prayer, I was on high alert spiritually when she was introduced to our team. Immediately, I noticed spiritual red flags when she introduced herself. After stating her name, she said, "I love Jesus, but I cuss a little. It's okay. I can cuss and still be saved and a Christian." While I commend her for being honest about where she was in her life, I could not accept that statement when it was cloaked in pride and acceptance.

Before the stones start flying my way, let's talk about this. Everyone should be honest about their mental, emotional, and spiritual states. Being honest with yourself and with God is a key to spiritual growth. Using that honesty to justify and accept behaviors or characteristics contrary to God's is absurd (James 3:10-12). You can identify which areas of your life need cleaning without justifying them as acceptable. God has called us to be holy and separate because He is holy (1 Peter 1:15-16) and to keep our mouths free of perversity (Proverbs 4:24).

If your definition of "holy" means perfect, sinless, or high and mighty, I challenge you to re-evaluate and redefine that word. Holiness requires a separateness that prevents us from intertwining with things that are spiritually corrupt and contrary to God. Also, it is *God's* Spirit that makes us holy, not us ourselves. God chose us and put His name and His glory on us. He alone is the one that makes us holy. The problem is that there are people who have a form of godliness but deny His power (2 Timothy 3:5). Do not be deceived by these people.

God already knows what you struggle with and He still loves you. He works on changing your heart and mind as much as you allow Him to, but He has never condoned or justified anything contrary to Him or His Spirit. Could you imagine if Jesus cussed out the Pharisees and Sadducees? Given His nature, it is difficult to envision because it'd be a contradiction! A lie is still a lie. The truth is still the truth. Wrong is still wrong. Right is still right. If the world accepts perverse speech and behavior as acceptable, and you also accept it as a believer, what difference is there between the two? You were called and chosen to be different, not to blend in like a beauty brush. Be the light, the city on a hill (Matthew 5:14-16); be the salt of the earth (v. 13).

To be clear, I was not judging her. I, too, had things I was asking God to help me clean up and pluck out. While I was not judging or condemning her, I did decide to test her. I knew what I discerned spiritually, but because she claimed to love God and to be His child, I decided to try the spirit to see if it was of God (1 John 4:1-5). So I gave her a chance.

After about a month and a half of her settling into her role as a supervisor, what I had initially picked up on spiritually started to manifest naturally. She disclosed private information about a coworker to me (though I did not ask, and there was no valid reason to tell me), she talked unfavorably about other departments, and she overstepped personal boundaries. I took mental notes of what I noticed, as I appeared to be the only one who noticed. I made sure not to get personal with her because she seemed unqualified to supervise.

In April of that year, about her fourth month of employment, I submitted a request for time off work. I knew it would be approved because of my work ethic alone and because I did not take off frequently. I requested time off to consecrate and participate in a Dominion Prayer Summit. It was the first time I had ever done something like this and the first time I saw spiritual attacks hit multiple areas and multiple people in a short time frame.

The Dominion Prayer Summit lasted three days, and the Spirit of the Lord was present all three days. There was no need to watch TV, get on social media, or talk on the phone. It was a time to fast, pray, sing praises, and get before the Lord. During these three days, the supervisor called me and texted me repeatedly. I did not respond until the end of the Prayer Summit because I was in consecration mode. Her messages implied that I had just not shown up for work and was not responding to her attempts to contact me. I waited before I replied because I have a problem with my character and work ethic being questioned without validity. When I finally responded, I reminded her that she previously approved my leave request. Instead of acknowledging the error made on her end, she requested to meet with me to discuss the incident when I returned to work. I noticed where the conversation was heading and shut it down with a simple reply of "Okay". I then went back into praise and worship mode. I was not about to get in my head or emotions when I just spent time in the presence of the Lord. Nope! Not today, satan!

I went to work that following Monday, and no meeting took place. When she rescheduled the meeting, she did not show up. I documented that and tucked it away for future reference. We then had a team meeting, in which she said out loud but in my direction, "When I call, I expect you all to answer." I would love to tell you what else was said, but I do not remember. I tuned her out and was silently praying in my head. I caught the subliminal dig toward me, but so did a few of my coworkers. They approached me after the meeting and told me they noticed her attitude toward me. They were not pleased, and I documented that for future reference as well.

Once again, she requested to meet with me. This time, though, I communicated with her through email so it would be date and time-stamped. She never replied. At this point, I thought I was tripping! *God, what did I do to her? Did I mean-mug her? Did I roll my eyes at her? What is this?* I then distanced myself to look at this situation with spiritual clarity. Distancing yourself from people can be detrimental to you and your relationships. Sometimes, however, the distance provides clarity by allowing you to see the bigger picture. I needed clarity, answers, and vindication because her actions toward me weren't making sense.

A few days went by, and we had another team meeting. I was physically present but had no desire to be there. I admit that what I did next was not the best idea. It was, however, strategic. I put an earbud into one ear, leaving the other free for me to listen. At the time, we were reviewing our policies and procedures for accuracy. My body posture and facial expressions communicated that I was not listening, but I was. I tried my best to stay grounded, as I did not like what I felt in the atmosphere. So, I started humming a gospel tune in my head. Doing this kept me focused and prevented me from saying what was on my mind.

The meeting ended, and she immediately requested to meet with me. I agreed but found my feet heading toward HR instead of her office. It felt as if I were not in my own body! At first, I was unaware of where I was going or why until someone asked, "Are you okay? You don't look like yourself." It took me a few seconds, but I was honest and explained what had just happened. Then I heard the Lord tell me to ask someone to sit in the meeting. I did not comprehend why He wanted me to do that, but I obeyed.

When I arrived at her office with a Human Resource representative, I noticed she was slightly surprised. She asked my coworker-friend to sit in the meeting but was not counting on me bringing someone. Let alone someone from HR. I repeatedly told myself to remain calm during that meeting. Even though *I* knew I hadn't done anything to warrant such an attitude from her, how I responded would make all the difference. There was some back and forth between us, but when she asked if I had a problem with her, I knew the true reason for her calling that meeting had been revealed.

She intended to fire me and have my coworker-friend there as a witness. Unfortunately for her, I threw that plan off by inviting an HR representative to sit in the meeting. She began grasping at something that was not there, making claims against my personality, character, and work ethic. She was reaching but had no basis for either claim she presented. While each statement she argued was unfounded, my counterpoints were documented and reinforced with witnesses.

At some point during the meeting, she appeared upset because what she originally planned did not work. She then mentioned that I had my earbuds in during the team meeting. She stated that I was not paying attention and being distracting. True, I did appear to be inattentive, but I countered that my coworkers were on their phones, laptops, or talking to each other. Thus, I could not have been the only person that was inattentive or distracting. I also repeated verbatim what the team discussed in the meeting and asked if I could do that had I not been paying attention. Was my remark smart-mouthed and sarcastic? Oh absolutely! It also stumped her because she couldn't refute it.

Then she went in for the kill: "It seems like you don't want to be here, and I don't need a cancer on my team. So you can leave." I slowly blinked twice to make sure I heard what I heard. Surely, she did not call me a cancer! Not me, whose paperwork got completed on time. Not me, who had great relationships with personnel from different departments. Not me, who had never raised my voice at her or treated her with hostility. She had to have mistaken me for a different Bree.

But she did call me a cancer. I heard it clearly, and so did everyone else in the room. I was livid, and my vision was tinting red! It took God, Jesus, the Holy Spirit, and all the Heavenly angels to stop me from jumping across her desk to make her eat those words. Whether cancer runs in someone's family or not, to compare someone to cancer is tasteless, classless, degrading, offensive, and flat-out disrespectful. I was fully prepared to happily go to jail that day, except I could not move. I envisioned myself sending her to meet the King, but I could not physically move to make that happen. And I heard God say, "That's what she wants. Be quiet. Be still." Ain't God good! It was *so* hard for me to be obedient! If I had not, though, I would not have seen God's hand in this situation.

HR then spoke up, interjected, and tried to get us to work toward a solution. I agreed to continue being professional, as I had been doing, but emphasized my desire for personal boundaries. The meeting ended, and I became aware that my body temp had risen. I was shaking and starting to see spots. I knew that I needed to distance myself immediately before someone got hurt. I needed to use the same coping skills that I teach in my therapy sessions.

I went to my office and called my prayer partner. I explained what happened and asked them to pray with and for me. Not even five minutes after we finished praying, HR called me for a debriefing. I was much calmer than I had been, but the incident was still fresh on my mind. HR informed me that the supervisor's claims were unsupported and unfounded, and mine were very much validated.

Won't He do it! "Praise the Lord, who has avenged the insult I received" (1 Samuel 25:39)! I wanted to cry rivers because it felt wonderful to be validated, especially after someone tried to attack my character and make false claims against me. In a journal entry I wrote on April 7, 2021, I asked the Lord to help me confuse the enemy and not give people the satisfaction of labeling me with their level of understanding of me. I then asked the Lord to be in the meeting with me so I could control myself and not say anything rude or harsh. God did exactly what I asked of Him! He kept my mouth from spewing venom and defended me like only He can. Much like the Lord responded to David in his time of distress, He responded to me. Praise the Lord!

Exodus 14:14 says, "The Lord Himself will fight for you. Just stay calm." Even though I wanted to snatch her by her edges and new growth, I was obedient when I heard the Lord tell me to be quiet and be still. It is necessary to have spiritual ears to hear what the Lord is saying. Had I not been spiritually sensitive, I would have missed hearing the Lord tell me to have someone to sit in the meeting. I would have also missed hearing the Lord tell me to be quiet and still so He could fight this battle for me.

Disobeying God is a serious offense (Deuteronomy 11:26-28; 1 Kings 13:20-22) and has dire consequences for the disobedient individual, their family, and their descendants. It eventually leads to death. Obedience, on the other hand, lays the groundwork for successful spiritual service. It holds a great reward. My obedience to the Lord's voice and instructions led to my vindication and put me in a position of favor (1 Samuel 15:22), both with God and with man.

I often admire how David, who also had favor with God and man, refrained from killing Saul. Even though Saul tried several times to kill him, David refused to raise a hand against Saul. In truth, David did nothing to sin against Saul; Saul was just jealous of the anointing in David that he no longer experienced. But just as David pointed out his innocence, which allowed Saul an opportunity to admit his wrong, this supervisor was allowed to apologize to me for her wrong.

She told HR that she did not realize she had compared me to cancer, even though I asked a clarifying question that she confirmed. I did not believe her response to HR because what is in your heart will surely come out of your mouth (Matthew 12:34). Even still, HR gave her 30 days to apologize. It was both generous and ridiculous of HR to extend that courtesy to her. If an apology is genuinely heartfelt, it does not take 30 days to express. I agreed, however, because I was honest in what I said about being professional, and I do not play about my character getting assassinated.

I had no hope that she would apologize, and I communicated as such to HR. 30 days passed, and she had yet to apologize. She had even started to avoid me. Honestly, I was not surprised and had even expected it to happen. God knew she wasn't going to apologize. I knew it. She knew it. My prayer partner knew it. The paint on the wall knew it. The grass growing between the sidewalk knew it. I called it for what it was, but it also showed HR and other personnel that she was not who she had claimed to be. I then refused to work under her "leadership", so I put in my notice to leave. I do believe that had I stayed, I would have seen God move even more on my behalf. I petitioned Him for something else instead, and He gave it. In reality, I was more afraid of what I would physically do to her, having to see and interact with the person who referenced me as cancer and had not apologized for it. For her safety, it was best that I left.

She did not last there too much longer. I was not surprised to hear the news and thanked God again for vindicating me. I am not saying any of this to gloat; I am cautioning you to be careful about who you speak against and who you mistreat. You are not speaking against or mistreating that person; they are simply representatives. The person you are mistreating is God. And He will respond to defend His name, His character, and the people that belong to Him.

Who God Says I Am

In addition to learning God's character and understanding your identity in Him (Belt of Truth), living honorably and guarding your heart against sin (Breastplate of Righteousness), and standing firm in your beliefs against every fiery dart (Shield of Faith), you must also put on the Helmet of Salvation. Similar to a regular helmet, the Helmet of Salvation protects our minds and thoughts. Positive and negative thoughts enter our minds daily, but not everyone dwells or acts on the negative. Rather, we are commissioned to "think about the things of heaven, not the things of earth" (Colossians 3:2), to "let God transform you into a new person by changing the way you think" (Romans 12:2), to "destroy every proud obstacle that keeps people from knowing God...capture their rebellious thoughts..." (2 Corinthians 10:5), and to "fix your thoughts on what is true, and honorable, and right, and pure, and lovely, and admirable. Think about things that are excellent and worthy of praise" (Philippians 4:8).

The reason why so many spiritual battles involve the mind is because the mind holds our conscious thinking and decision-making. It is akin to the heart, not the brain. The heart is the seat of our emotions, thoughts, intentions, and motives. It houses our character and is the most vital part of our being. If the enemy can capture your thoughts, he can also capture your emotions, actions, and character. Do not let the enemy trap you in this manner, for anyone whose character reflects that of the devil will be cut off (Matthew 7:17-20).

If you struggle with taking your thoughts captive, ask the Holy Spirit to help you. He is a willing Helper and Guide that we all need. There were several times I wrestled with having positive thoughts about that supervisor, even after I left. I acknowledged it by saying, "God, You've got to help me with this! I want to call her out and talk bad to her! I need Your help." The Holy Spirit has since helped me to release my thoughts about her. I was able to renew my mind and focus back on things that were good, pure, and holy. I also asked God to replace my mind with His (Philippians 2:5).

How often have negative thoughts taken our minds captive, whether we think them about ourselves or others? The thoughts you have can significantly impact your life for better or worse. If you believe in your heart that you are a failure or unworthy, your emotions and behaviors will follow suit. Likewise, if I had believed in my heart that I was a cancer, I would have become one. What you think and believe in your heart about yourself does matter (Proverbs 23:7). You simply need to know what is true and what is false. Remember, it is okay to be honest with yourself and God about where you are. He already knows, but your acknowledgment and surrendered heart are equally important. Be honest with God and allow Him to change you with His Holy Spirit.

When you put on the Helmet of Salvation, you are protecting your mind with the assurance that God has given. There are numerous assurances the Lord has afforded to us! What matters is which one you choose to believe and stand on. Any thought that goes against the assurances of God should be taken captive immediately and refuted with the Word of God. For those dealing with negative self-talk and beliefs in your heart—whether it's your words or words someone spoke over you—I challenge you to spend more time getting to know yourself through God's eyes. Then, use these positive Biblical affirmations to challenge the enemy and those negative thoughts. Here are some of my own that I use:

I am chosen, holy, and loved (Colossians 3:12)

I am forgiven (1 John 2:12; 14)

I am a child of God (1 John 3:1-2)

I am an ambassador for Christ (2 Corinthians 5:20)

I am loved, valuable, and worth it (John 3:16; 1 John 4:10-13)

I am more than a conqueror (Romans 8:37) *

I am strong (2 Corinthians 12:10)

I am not an accident or a mistake (Ephesians 1:4-5)

I am capable (Philippians 4:13)

I am His masterpiece (Ephesians 2:10)

I am fearfully and wonderfully made (Psalms 139:14)

I am well-designed. I have power and authority. I am good (Genesis 1:26-31) *

I marked my two favorite affirmations with asterisks. Through everything I have experienced, I am more than a conqueror through Jesus Christ. I wholeheartedly believe that without Jesus, my life would not be remotely close to what it is now. I also enjoy reminding myself and the devil of my position: I am a little lower than the angels and crowned with glory and honor (Psalms 8:5). I have power and authority from God over the enemy. I am not defenseless. I am not a cancer. I am well-designed. I am good!

Prayer

I bring every negative thought into captivity by the power of the Holy Spirit. I rebuke every word curse spoken over my life, whether from my mouth or the mouth of someone else. The power those word curses have held over me is broken in the name of Jesus! Holy Spirit, help me to guard my tongue and to speak life over myself and into myself. I pray that my mind, heart, eyes, and ears are open to receive what You think about me, how You feel about me, and how You see me. Lord, heal every area affected by those word curses and help me to cling to who You say I am, which You have confirmed in Your Word: I am a child of God. I am loved with an unfailing love. I am valuable. I have a purpose. And I am a formidable foe against the enemy. In Jesus' name, Amen.

Sword of the Spirit

Purposeful Testing

Are you still with me? If so, you are familiar with the spiritual attacks on my mind and emotions. There were several times I mentally kicked my 11-year-old self. You just had to ask God for a test! Now look, the tests keep coming, and they won't stop! All jokes aside, I have discovered that my testing serves multiple purposes.

First, to reveal what's in me. I hear several people comment on my level of patience, and I always silently laugh. If only they knew me some years ago! The testing I have undergone has helped me to develop and strengthen my patience (James 1:2-4). If people notice I am patient, it is because God has given me more of His patience. If people notice I am wise, it is because God has given me more of His wisdom. I would not consider myself to be the most patient or wise person. However, if that is what people notice, then I thank God for working on me in those areas. It is always a good feeling when others can see more of His attributes in me rather than my own.

Second, to perfect my obedience to Him and His statutes. I have deliberately disobeyed God more times than I care to count. His Word, however, says that those who love Him also obey His commands (John 14:15). I had to align my words with my actions of obedience. Thankfully, I have repented of that wickedness, and God has not held a record against me. His love is unconditionally perfect, and His grace is sufficient.

Third, to be better equipped than I was before. I do not always pass my tests the first time around. Sometimes, depending on the situation, it may take me three or four times to pass that test. That usually happens when I am warring against the Spirit with my flesh and being stubborn. Despite this, whenever I have failed a test, God revealed how He would have me respond instead. I would repent, of course, and then do as instructed.

Outside of being tempted by the desires of flesh, there are a few reasons why most people do not pass their tests. Most do not read their Bible consistently. Some do not understand what they have read. Still, others do not apply what they have read. Reading the Word of God—the Bible—is imperative for your spiritual walk. It is a conditioning tool, removing the gunk and grime of sin while giving you a more polished look. The Word of God will teach you about God's character, increase your faith, and renew your mind. It will also help you to understand God's will. There are many other reasons why reading the Word of God is important, but I cannot list them all right here. Regardless, this tool is a mighty weapon against the enemy.

Do not make excuses when it comes to reading the Word. There are 24 hours in each day, subtracting 8 hours for a recommended night's rest and 8 hours for the average work day. That still leaves 8 hours to read at least one verse or chapter. My Apostle often mentions that if you do not open up a physical Bible to read, then at least listen to it audibly. The goal is to ensure you create a daily habit of reading the Word of God by any means necessary.

After you read or listen to the Word of God, then meditate on it. Doing so will help to increase your comprehension of Scripture. One of the earliest verses I learned to memorize was John 3:16. I could rapidly quote this verse but did not understand the depth of what it entailed. I now understand this verse better because I allowed the words to sink into my heart. I meditated on it and studied it.

Studying the Word requires that you comprehend the context of what you read. I admit I did not always understand the Old Testament scriptures when I read them. I would bypass Numbers, Deuteronomy, and Judges because the contents were intimidating. Not to mention, I struggled with reading the King James Version. There was a fix for that, though. I started reading versions of the Bible that were better for my level of comprehension. I then found myself studying the Old Testament with deep respect. Get a version of the Bible that works for you and your comprehension level, not anyone else's.

But do not stop there. You have built a consistent Bible-reading lifestyle, great! You have got a version of the Bible that you understand, awesome! Now what? Reading, comprehending, and memorizing scriptures is a great starting point but not a destination. You must apply what you have read by putting it into action.

Were you aware that the devil knows Scripture as well? He can quote it beautifully, too! Yet his tongue is deceptive, twisting the truth (the Word of God) to fit his own agenda. The best example of applying the Word of God comes from Jesus Himself. In Matthew 4:1-11, Jesus was tempted by the devil in the wilderness. The devil misquoted Scripture, attempting to appeal to Jesus. Jesus, however, applied the Word of God effectively, which caused satan to flee. Jesus also went up against the Pharisees and Sadducees, who claimed to know the Word better than the Word Himself (Matthew 12:1-14). Do not be misled by those who claim to know Scripture but teach religion over sound doctrine. This is yet another reason why it is important to know the Word and continuously study and meditate on it day and night (Joshua 1:8). Let it get down deep in your heart so it will be displayed in your words and actions. This is what it means to take up the Sword of the Spirit.

Stand on the Word

During the summer of 2023, I was reminded of the power of the Sword of the Spirit. My flesh was warring with the Spirit, and I was conflicted about the best way to handle a difficult situation. God instructed me not to worry about it, which was very difficult for me to do. My emotions were heightened, and I wanted to handle things my way. That did not last very long. Eventually, I had to return and stand on the words God spoke to me and the Scriptures concerning how I felt.

During that summer, my daddy died a month before his birthday. He spoke with me regarding dying, but the actual moment was no less melancholy. A lot of people thought his transition took a heavy toll on me, but actually, it was dealing with his relatives that affected me. Death and grief have a way of making people act weird. In some cases, it reveals their true character.

My dad's last remaining sibling had taken over, making medical arrangements without asking either of his children if they agreed, if they needed help, or what they wanted done. I thought that behavior was odd because my dad and his sibling had not spoken in quite some time. Honestly, his sibling did not even know he had been in the hospital for a little over two months. I was bothered but held my peace because God told me not to worry about the situation.

Right before my dad lost his ability to speak, he called to share some information with me. The call flat-out disturbed me, and I fought back tears until he finished what he had to tell me. When we got off the phone, I immediately went to God. I learned to take fights to the spirit realm instead of the natural from my previous tests. I was binding and rebuking every spirit of witchcraft from his hospital room. I prayed that God would dispatch angels to watch over him, as I could not be physically present. I also prayed for peaceful rest for his soul. After I prayed, I stood on the Word. I had to trust God in what He had to say about this situation.

A few days later, God showed me a vision of my dad transitioning. God told me, "After you speak to him, he'll be gone." Sure enough, that's what happened. I called the facility, and the nurse transferred me to his room. The nurse graciously held the phone to his ear while I spoke. He could not talk back, but he could hear. It was emotionally painful to talk to him that way, but I was glad I did. My dad did not have an immediate transition, but he did transition after we spoke. Aside from the nurses and doctors, I was the last familial voice he heard.

I was sad but super grateful. I found solace in the fact that not everything went according to the plans of others. My dad's sibling had planned for some relatives to say their final goodbyes to him in person before he died, which he did not want. My dad told at least three people what he wanted for the end of his life, but because no one consulted with his children, his wishes were ignored.

When I tell you that the spirit of Peter rose fiercely on the inside of me! I was ready to slice and dice somebody, both physically and spiritually. I thought about traveling to the "funeral services" and fighting those involved on sight! It would have dishonored his memory and wishes had I attended, so I decided against it.

Then I thought about cursing them, their children, their children's children, and their children's children's children. I was fuming!

That's when my Apostle called me. It's so funny because, a lot of times, I feel like she can sense me in the Spirit. We talked for a bit, and I heard the words in my head even as she spoke them to me: "You have to forgive them and pray for them." I knew I had to, but that didn't mean I wanted to. I hadn't felt rage like that in a while. I was hot all over, even to the point where my head was hurting. But my Apostle was right. I did need to forgive them and pray for them.

So I did. I prayed for anyone who mistreated my dad, whether they were hospital workers or related to him. I prayed against every lie spoken against his name, every act of deception, and any trace of malice or ill-intent during the time that he was in the hospital. I prayed for God to have mercy on them and to show them the offense they caused. I, again, had to go back and rely on what God had spoken to me. He told me not to worry about the situation. I had to stand in faith that He had it under control.

A day later, I scrolled across a few Facebook posts about my dad. I was reminded of how his wishes had been ignored, and the anger came back. The irritation came back. The unforgiveness came back! My heart began to harden, and I struggled to let it go. You do not grow up thinking that someone you are related to would do something shady, but I had to remind myself that not all relatives are family. You could be related to someone by DNA; it would still not make you family. Jacob and Esau were twin brothers, but their descendants—the Israelites and Edomites—were not planning family reunions together. Instead, the Edomites were enemies of the Israelites, and the two nations warred against each other for quite some time.

In my mind, I knew that warring against my relatives was not the answer. My heart, however, was not arriving at the same conclusion. To keep myself from sinning while angry, I found positive ways to distract my mind. I would sing gospel songs, talk to God, pray, write in my journal, read my Bible, and watch funny videos. One day, I stumbled across a video that a Christian comedian posted about drop-kicking people in the throat when they mistreat you. I watched that video countless times and laughed so hard because I could relate! The video ended with a reminder to show love and to forgive people even when they mistreat you. It was not what I wanted to hear, but it was Biblical. So, I prayed a prayer of forgiveness after watching that video.

I then found myself reading Matthew 18:21-22. I laugh every time I read this section of the chapter because Peter was trying to limit how often he forgave someone. I only have to forgive seven times, right, Lord? Then Jesus, with His wise self, responded by saying seventy times seven (490 times). Even with this number, you'd have to be off your rocker to keep count of how many times you have forgiven someone. And what would be the point? I know for a fact that God has forgiven me way more than that, and He has yet to keep a record. I ask Him to throw my sins into the sea of forgetfulness (Micah 7:18-19) and remember them no more (Jeremiah 31:34b; Hebrews 10:17). I then pray Psalms 51 sincerely as I repent and ask for restoration.

So, as much as I do not want to forgive people when they hurt me, I know I have to. Yes, it is for my mental and emotional well-being. It is also because it's God's instructions. Matthew 6:14-15 tells us that if we forgive others, God will forgive us; if we do not forgive others, God will not forgive us. So, if God can forgive me for my sins, I can work to forgive others. It may not always be as simple and easy as saying, "I forgive you. Let's be buddy-buddy." No, your thoughts and emotions related to the event need time and space to heal. Sometimes, that can take a minute, but the principle works! Standing on the Word works!

How can you stand on the Word of God if you do not comprehend it? The Sword of the Spirit is made up of three components: consistent reading (or listening) of the Word, understanding the Word, and applying the Word. You need all three for this weapon to have its greatest effect against the enemy. Even though I was pissed off, I still had to apply the Word in this situation. I still had to trust God when He told me not to worry. The Sword of the Spirit (the Word of God) is a powerful tool to use in moments of uncertainty, distress, sadness, and more. Read it, study it, and apply it.

<u>Prayer</u>

Lord, Your Word is true, and it will accomplish all that You please. It will prosper where You send it and will not return void. Holy Spirit, help me to be more disciplined in reading and studying the Word of God. I want to be better equipped so I am not easily tricked and deceived by the enemy or false teachers. Help me remember what I study so I can use it when and where necessary. Help me to understand what I read, and I will hide it in my heart. I will use the Word of God in times of uncertainty, distress, and testing. This Sword will help me to resist the devil and his tactics but also emerge from such situations victoriously. I am a victor because You have declared me victorious. And I am purposing to put Your Word into practice. In Jesus' name, Amen.

SANDALS OF PEACE

It's Bigger Than You

Even after praying for my relatives and working on forgiving them, I realized that I was still holding on to this thought: *How can someone you're related to do something like this?* I could not get past it. God began to deal with me about going deeper. It was bigger than my thoughts about the situation. It was bigger than how I felt about the situation. It was bigger than me, period.

This entire book focuses on spiritual warfare, which requires your vision to transcend beyond the natural. Yes, it hurt to have relatives do inconsiderate things, but it was deeper than that. Look at what is going on spiritually! Anything that has a basis or foundation in a unified covenant relationship with God is automatically on the enemy's radar to be divided and conquered. That is why relationships, marriages, friendships, business relationships, and family relationships are heavily attacked. When the union expresses ministry or covenant partnership, the enemy will do his best to attack it and break it apart. For this reason, you must remember the significance or purpose of your union or covenant partnership.

Take, for instance, the incident in Genesis 11. All the people in the world at that time spoke the same language. They came up with the idea of building a tower that reached the sky (Genesis 11:1-4). Their being unified without bickering, arguing, or killing each other was beautiful. Their motives for unifying, however, were not. It is not enough just to come together and be unified. Even demonic spirits can be unified in their plans to attack the people of God. No, your motive for unifying matters. When we unite in prayer, praise, worship, glorifying and honoring our Heavenly Father, God is with us and His presence can be easily felt. That's the power of being one-minded or on one accord for a divine purpose. Be sure that whatever union or partnership you find yourself in glorifies God, not yourself, someone else, or something else.

There is one Body and one Spirit; one Lord, one Faith, one Baptism; and one God and Father of all (Ephesians 4:4-6). We are to be united in the Spirit (Ephesians 4:3), to be one (John 17:21), and to live in harmony with each other (1 Corinthians 1:10). If anything has to do with Spiritual unification, harmony, or peace, it is of God. Where there is dissension, discord, hostility, and selfish ambition, there you will find flesh. Flesh and Spirit do not mix! They are oil and water, hot and cold.

The enemy—your enemy—will try to take the heat off himself and place it on flesh and blood. But that's not the kind of war we are fighting. You are not going to want to hear this, and I did not want to be reminded of this, but the truth is the truth: Your relatives are not the enemy. Your exes are not the enemy. Your supervisor is not the enemy. Yes, you can acknowledge that what they said and did was foul, disrespectful, inconsiderate, or hurtful. After you have acknowledged that, take the fight to the devil. Go from the natural to the spiritual.

That anger you feel toward another human? Take it out on the true enemy, the devil. You feel like drop-kicking somebody in the throat? Go drop-kick the devil. You want to gut-punch someone and knock the wind out of them? Go gut-punch the devil. You really want to snatch somebody by their edges and new growth? Go snatch the devil! Seriously, turn the tables back on him!

Do you think he cares if we kill each other? No! That's less work for him and part of what he wants anyway. Do you think he is bothered when anger rises and takes over? No! The angrier you are, the less inclined you are to listen (James 1:19), especially to wisdom (Proverbs 29:11). Do you think he is the least bit concerned about you if you sin? No! Sin that is left unrepented will lead to death (James 1:15; Romans 6:23), which is his endgame.

Spiritual Avenger

Think of the devil as an invisible Thanos and you are an avenger. This spiritual war does not only concern you and your family. It affects every living, breathing human on earth. It concerns every nation, nationality, race, and ethnicity. Spiritual warfare occurs in the following domains: religion, family, education, government, business, media, and arts and entertainment. I assure you that as you contemplate these areas, you will be able to identify a few wicked, corrupt, or evil practices.

Let's focus on religion since I mentioned it first. The spiritual warfare that takes place within this domain is one of confusion, blindness, and apostasy. I have seen people who claim to be Christians but who also practice tarot reading, spiritual readings, fortune telling, divination, or anything remotely similar. They try to convince others that white magic or black magic is harmless and okay. They also try to convince others that they know God and are still followers of God. Baby, deception is real! Whether or not they have been deceived, do not let yourself be deceived. None of that is of God!

If someone claims, "I know God," but doesn't obey God's commandments, that person is a liar and is not living in the truth. But those who obey God's word truly show how completely they love him. That is how we know we are living in him. Those who say they live in God should live their lives as Jesus did. (1 John 2:4-6)

I have never read in my Bible where Jesus practiced tarot readings or divination. It would have caused Him to be a contradiction or a hypocrite, neither of which is in His nature to be. Likewise, the children of God are also cautioned to stay away from such practices.

Deuteronomy 18:9-14 informs us that the Israelites would occupy the land of those who practiced fortune-telling, sorcery, witchcraft, casting spells, and calling on the spirits of the dead. God was removing those nations from the land because it was His to begin with, and He'd promised it to the descendants of Abraham, Isaac, and Jacob (Israel). The other reason was such practices were and still are detestable to the Lord. Jesus didn't come to do away with the law but to fulfill it (Matthew 5:17), so it still applies.

For those who try to say that tarot reading, fortune-telling, witchcraft, and other occult practices are the same as prophesying, you are sadly mistaken. I rebuke that lie in the name of Jesus! True prophets hear the voice of God Himself—the creator of Heaven and earth, the Alpha and Omega, Yahweh. They speak His words and not those of their own or some other spirit. Those who engage in occult practices do so by a spirit that is not God's and which is also limited in power. So, no, it is not the same thing.

For example, consider what happened in 1 Kings 18 after Israel split into two kingdoms, Israel and Judah. Ahab had married Jezebel, who killed the prophets of the Lord and instituted "prophets" of baal and asherah. Elijah, one of the true prophets of God at that time, asked the people how long they would hop between God and baal. "If the Lord is God, then follow Him" (1 Kings 18:21). He then orchestrated a contest between baal and God so that all the people could distinguish between the truth and deception. The "proph-a-liars" of baal danced, sang, chanted, and cut themselves as a way to get their god to respond to them. Their god never responded.

Elijah, on the other hand, had them pour water on the altar he rebuilt. He asked them to do this three times so the altar could be saturated with water. He wanted them to see that no magic or witchcraft was involved, only the power of the Lord. When he prayed, God sent fire to consume everything on that altar, including all the water. What a miraculous sign to witness!

Guess what happened next? The people who had strayed away from God and had gotten entangled with other spirits and occult practices had to re-acknowledge the Lord as supreme with their mouths. They then knew with certainty that no idol or deity held a candle to His power. Then those false prophets of baal were executed immediately!

A lot of these occult practices are subtle and not very blatant. The deception may be cloaked in words or phrases like "There's nothing wrong with it," "I thought it was fun," or "It's harmless." It is not. I do not say this to attack anybody, to put them down, or even to judge them. But the truth is the truth! What some people think is fun, cute, or harmless is a gateway, door, or even a portal to demonic and satanic practices. Do not be deceived.

I do not want to dwell too much on this topic. There is so much information on what most people know as the "7 Mountains That Influence Culture". I do not have the space to cover it extensively in this book. There are, however, several men and women who have studies available, backed up with scripture and used appropriately. You can find many of these teachings on YouTube.

Regardless of any entanglements you have found yourself in, repentance is an option. When Jonah finally delivered the message of the Lord to the city of Nineveh, the people repented. Everyone, from the king down to the lowest citizen, put on burlap and sat on ashes. And when God saw their repentance, He changed His mind regarding their destruction (Jonah 3). This is an example of the power of repentance. You can move the hand of God.

True repentance is a denunciation of sin, a proactively changing mind and heart, and a gift of God (2 Timothy 2:25). It can have a positive, life-changing effect on you and your family. We are all given opportunities to repent and return, but not everyone takes advantage of those opportunities. One of the worst things you could ever do is not repent at all. Despite whatever misstep or mistake you made, repent! The Lord will forgive you and cleanse you if you confess your sins to Him (1 John 1:9). Do not allow your heart to become so hardened that you fall prey to the dark abyss of hell simply because you will not repent.

God is not some terrible monster waiting to rain down hellfire and brimstone on you. If anything, His strongest desires are to have intimacy with His people, to have them repent, and to have them return unto Him (2 Chronicles 7:14). That does not sound like someone who is out to kill you anytime you mess up or make a mistake. No, that sounds like the good, patient, and loving Father that He is. The Good News is that God will welcome your repentant heart with open arms. He will not bring up your errors like people will do. He is kind and gentle, faithful and forgiving, loving and merciful. He is the best Father I have ever known.

This chapter may be a little shorter than the others, but it is because the entire book relates to this chapter. Sandals of Peace focuses on witnessing or evangelizing, sharing the Good News of salvation and freedom from sin, and standing firm in the confidence of our position. I do not witness or evangelize in the traditional sense, but I have not held back in sharing my experiences with God, Jesus, and the Holy Spirit with others. I have done so at church, school, work, in stores, and on social media. I have shared with believers and non-believers. Some have chosen to unfriend me and that is okay. It is their right to do so, but it does not stop me from sharing.

As you learn how to put on the full armor of God and use it properly, do not forget to teach others how to do the same. Share this with others; do not keep it to yourself. It is my hope and prayer that scales be removed and veils be torn so that more people can see what is going on spiritually.

Prayer

Father God, remove the scales from my eyes so that I may see spiritually! Tear the veil and help me to see and understand clearly. If I have fallen into the trap of deception, reveal it to me. Rescue me with Your Truth, and I will be free! Then, use me to help free others. Lord, as I witness and evangelize to others, help me not get discouraged when some reject me. Remind me that they rejected You first. Strengthen me to stand firm in the confidence of my position and not be swayed by what is culturally acceptable or popular. As much as possible, help me to live in peace with everyone while maintaining fidelity in sharing the Good News. In Jesus' name, Amen.

WAGING WAR IS A LIFESTYLE

Spiritual Retaliation

I would love to tell you that waging war against the enemy or engaging in spiritual battles will bring a lasting, peaceful result. It would not be entirely true. Much like in a natural war, there is often retaliation or recoil. Even the Israelites had peace for some time before going to war again. Engaging in spiritual warfare is not a one-and-done type of action. It is continuous. It is a lifestyle.

I experienced a lot of spiritual retaliation during the writing process of this book. Several of my pens stopped working suddenly (new pens, too), negative thoughts popped into my mind like popcorn kernels under heat, and distractions were coming from everywhere. These may not seem like retaliation tactics, but they are. Even as I researched ways to format a book, I heard this thought: "Your book won't sell. You don't even have enough pages to sell a book. Just look, your book is nowhere near that [other] book." Doubt started creeping into my mind, and I immediately went to God.

I was talking to God, once again being honest about my thoughts and feelings. Then I heard God say, "Why are you upset?" *Ouch! Okay then, God.* I didn't bother to wait for His next response because His words had a "finalization" tone paired with them. In other words, I needed to finish what He told me to do and not worry about anything else. See, the devil did not want this book to be published! He didn't want those who read this book to be aware of the contents within. Sorry, not sorry, but I had a mandate from God to get this book out. What God has spoken, anointed, or mandated to be, it shall be.

Other retaliation tactics used against me included seeing shadowy figures in my places of residence, feeling the presence of darkness and death, waking up with red marks on my skin (usually around my arms or chest area), and attacking my body with illness. Some of these methods were intimidation tactics used only to scare me. Other methods were used to eliminate my existence. For over a month, I had difficulty breathing, even though X-rays showed that my lungs were clear. I could not inhale a full breath, but medically, nothing was wrong with me.

One night, I was so tired that I fell asleep on my back. Even though it's one of the recommended sleeping positions, I am not a fan. I woke up in the middle of the night, and panic hit me immediately. I couldn't breathe! I was gasping for air like a fish out of water! I tried to sit up or roll over, but I couldn't. It was like someone was holding down my lungs while sitting on top of me. It felt like drowning alive, except there was no water. Then, suddenly, I felt a great force in my back. *Whoosh!* I could feel myself being flipped over on my side, but it wasn't me doing it. When I was flipped over on my side, I felt the grip loosen from my front, and I was able to inhale air. It was a hard inhale—the kind that hurts your chest—but I didn't care. I was just happy to be able to breathe! I cried and praised God greatly that night because that could have been it for me. But I am still here by His grace, mercy, lovingkindness, and watchful protection over my life. Thank You, Lord, for fighting on my behalf!

And God fights for you, too. If God showed us how much He protects us, covers us, and shields us from many spiritual attacks, we would have an even deeper love, respect, and appreciation for Him. Even the Holy Spirit intercedes for us with groanings that cannot be expressed in words (Romans 8:26-27). Oh, how He loves us! I am so honored to not only be a servant but a child of the Most High. My Father in Heaven loves me so much that He sent His son to die in my place, even while I was still a sinner (John 3:16; Romans 5:8). The same is true for you, too. Jesus died for all: believer and nonbeliever, persecutor and praiser, whore and worshiper.

Everyone—Black, White, Hispanic, Jew, Greek, Italian—has been extended an opportunity to enter into salvation by faith through Jesus Christ (Isaiah 45:22; 1 Timothy 2:3-4). Not everyone believes or accepts Christ, however, which ultimately is a rejection of Him. We are all given a choice: to accept or reject

Him. When we accept Him, we die out to the desires of our flesh and have access to eternal life (Romans 6:12-23; 1 John 5:20-21). When we reject Him, we act according to flesh and sin, and we bring judgment on ourselves (John 16:8-11). We then will not experience eternal life but instead remain under God's judgment (John 3:36). Whether or not you accept Him or reject Him now, there will come a time when every knee will bow, and every tongue confess that He alone is Lord (Romans 14:11; Philippians 2:10-11).

Spiritual Agreements

I have discovered that it is difficult to wage war against something you agree with. When you have aligned yourself with something, you tend to view it as acceptable, okay, right, and so on. For years, I saw nothing wrong with the amount of Coca-Cola I consumed. It was my favorite drink, and I indulged in it whenever I wanted to. It held the same significance for me that alcohol and weed holds for others. My doctor at the time warned me of the adverse effects the excessive consumption had on my kidneys, but I continued drinking it. I convinced myself that drinking it was harmless, so my attempts to stop were futile.

At the beginning of 2021, my church instituted a corporate Daniel Fast. We were asked to give up meat, sweets, and sodas for 21 days. I desired to be free from drinking Coca-Cola all the time and committed to fasting from it. Since that fast, I have not had a drop of Coca-Cola. I mainly drink water, juice, and, occasionally, a Sprite. Even when presented with the opportunity to drink Coca-Cola again, I found that my desire to do so was no longer present. I was free! When you genuinely desire to be released from something and are no longer entertaining it, God will break whatever connection exists.

This applies to alcohol and drugs, other addictions, having sex when you're unmarried (fornication), sleeping with others outside of your marriage (adultery), habitually lying, cussing like it's a separate language, and so on. When you are no longer in agreement with these things and desire to be released from them, humbly repent, fast, and pray for God to sever the spiritual connection to them. Granted, some of these may require the help of a professional such as a licensed therapist, but the general idea is that as you fast, you decrease the dominion your flesh has and increase the dominion of the Spirit. It is a sacrifice to give up what your flesh desires so that you can receive what God desires for you. Many do not want to make that sacrifice. Sadly, they will go no further than where they are currently because of it.

If I agree that there is nothing wrong with telling a lie here or a lie there, I might not pray against the spirit of deception. If I agree that there is nothing wrong with dirty jokes or cussing because "God knows my heart," then I'm not going to seek deliverance from it. If I agree that people should be with whoever or whatever, I'm not going to rebuke spiritual perversity that involves sexual sin. Such sexual sin is actually in violation of God's creative intention: human with human, man with woman, and to leave married people alone!

Oftentimes, the attack is against the person who engages in such sinful acts rather than the perverse spirit behind such acts. I mentioned before that people are not your true enemy. The devil is. He relishes in everything wicked, evil, sinful, and morally corrupt. He opposes everything about God, including the purposes of God's creation. The attacks should be against the spirit of deception and perversity, not the human host of such things. Change your battleground. Change your strategy. Change the outcome.

Rescue others by snatching them from the flames of judgment. Show mercy to still others, but do so with great caution, hating the sins that contaminate their lives. (Jude 1: 23)

There are agreements in other areas that have brought the judgment of the Lord upon the earth, such as removing God and putting idols in His place. America has a phrase on its currency that states, "In God, we trust." Yet, God and prayer have been removed from public schools that are funded by our federal government. How can you claim to be a nation under God that also trusts in God, yet you have removed the very essence of Him to make room for other deities? Not only that, but several states have demonic structures erected as monuments, symbolizing a public declaration of influence and servitude to that idol.

Around 2018, there was some controversy in Little Rock due to a satanic-worshiping group that wanted to erect a statue of baphomet on the state capitol grounds. Spiritually, it was an act of defiance and rebellion against God. I commend the senator who spoke out against it at the time. He took a bold stand to leave the Ten Commandments statue alone, without any idols erected on state capitol grounds. Whether people recognized this act as a spiritual attack or not, it was. For this reason, it is important to see things spiritually and attack them there so you will also know how to handle them in the natural, physical world.

As quickly as they brought that structure in, it was gone. It reminded me of what happened when the Philistines captured the Ark of the Covenant and placed it beside their idol, dagon. That little idol broke, and the hand of the Lord was against them, making them eager to return the Ark of the Covenant to Israel. Idol worship does exist; it just looks more modernized than in ancient Israeli times. God's stance on idol worship has not changed. It is still considered foolish to worship something man-made (Isaiah 44:9-20, 45:16), especially when all idols will completely disappear (Isaiah 2:18).

If you have come into an agreement with anything that exalts itself against the power and knowledge of God, I pray that it is revealed and broken in the name of Jesus! I close every door, gate, window, or portal access given to the enemy. From this day forward, his access has been denied! I stand in proxy, asking God to forgive us for entering into an agreement with the kingdom of darkness and for erecting idols in His place, whether physically or spiritually. May the Spirit of Truth reveal all areas where an agreement has been made, and may the fire of the Holy Spirit sever that agreement and connection in the name of Jesus! Lord, exchange our hearts and minds for Your own. Create in us a clean heart, O Lord, and renew a right spirit within us. Purify us with hyssop, and we will be clean; wash us, and we will be whiter than snow. Then we will teach others Your ways, and they will turn to You (Psalm 51). I stand in agreement that it is so. In Jesus' name, Amen.

As I mentioned previously, repentance is an option. It is God's will that no one perishes but walks in repentance (1 Peter 3:9b). We also have Jesus as our advocate if we do sin (1 John 2:1). This is important because He became the sacrifice or atonement for the whole world. He is the ultimate stain remover, making us holy and clean without a spot or wrinkle.

If you are not saved and desire to be, do not wait any longer. You do not have to wait to attend church on Sunday to be saved. You can do that right now. Romans 10:9 tells us, "If you openly declare that Jesus is Lord and believe in your heart that God raised Him from the dead, you will be saved."

Repeat this out loud:

Father, I confess that I have sinned against You. I ask that You forgive me of all of my sins. I invite You into my heart and give You permission to change my life. I believe that You gave Your one and only son as ransom for my sins. I believe that Jesus Christ died in my place on the cross, was buried, and was resurrected. I believe that You, Lord, by the power of Your Holy Spirit, raised Christ from the dead so that I may have eternal life. And because I believe that with my heart and have openly confessed it with my mouth, I am saved! In Jesus' name, Amen!

I rejoice with every one of you who has just accepted Christ into your life by making a bold declaration of faith in Him. You are now ambassadors, representing someone and something much bigger than yourself. Will you get it right every time? No. Neither do I. Will it be super easy and relaxing? No. I have tried to quit many times before and have lost count. Will you sometimes struggle with your past self as you learn to embrace your God-given identity? Yes. The enemy will not let you go without a fight. Will it be worth it in the end? Absolutely! I cannot begin to fully describe it because "eyes have not yet seen and ears have not yet heard all of what God has prepared for those who love Him" (1 Corinthians 2:8-10).

Conclusion

Misusing the Armor

I do have to caution that when the armor of God is not properly used or executed, there is potential for spiritual interference to occur. Examples of this are making foolish vows as Japheth did (Leviticus 5:4-5), abusing grace (Romans 6:1-2), tolerating sin, refusing to forgive others, and more. Without proper execution of the armor of God, you leave yourself open to spiritual attacks. The devil does not play fair, but you don't have to either. You have access to heavy artillery—God, Jesus, the Holy Spirit, and angels that will war on your behalf.

The weapons we have access to make all the difference between a natural lightweight and a spiritual heavyweight. Handle them responsibly. Do not diminish the power of God's armor by using only a portion of it or misusing it altogether. You will not be able to resist the enemy in times of evil unless you use all the pieces together: the Belt of Truth, the Breastplate of Righteousness, the

Sandals of Peace, the Shield of Faith, the Helmet of Salvation, and the Sword of the Spirit. Each piece of armor has a different purpose and function, but they all work together like the Body of Christ (1 Corinthians 12:12-27).

Right Now Assignment

As believers, we have a right-now assignment outlined in 1 Corinthians 16:13-14: "Be on guard, stand firm in the faith, be courageous, be strong, and do everything with love." To "be on guard" means that we need to be alert, watchful, and ready to respond. You must stay alert and watch out for the devil, who "prowls around like a roaring lion" (1 Peter 5:8). This is not the time to be like a gazelle, skipping through life unaware. No, this is the time to be a lion yourself, "daring the enemy to rouse you" (Genesis 49:9).

To "stand firm in the faith" means to be steadfast, immovable, or unwavering (Hebrews 11:1-13). To "be courageous" means to not be easily discouraged by unfavorable circumstances (Joshua 1:6-9). In 2021, I started the process of buying a home. I got discouraged when financing fell through and the sellers backed out. But I heard God say, "That wasn't the house," which my Apostle confirmed shortly after. It was disappointing, but I stood firm that God knows best and desires the best for me. That disappointment was soon replaced with expectancy!

"Be strong" means to use great force, withstand pressure, and be firmly established. No matter how much weight you can deadlift or how many muscles you have, you are powerless against the enemy without strength and power from God. His strength is both nourishing and powerful, a shield and a spear.

"Do everything with love" is self-explanatory. Love is defined in 1 Corinthians 13:4-8. It is the foundation of who God is and how He operates. You can be the most famous person in the world and have all the money your heart desires, but if you cannot love like how 1 Corinthians 13:4-8 tells us how to love, then you have nothing and you are nothing. "Three things will last forever—faith, hope, and love—and the greatest of these is love" (1 Corinthians 13:13).

I Declare War

I now see why Paul was so passionate in his writings. He aimed to educate, empower, encourage, enlighten, and equip the people of God. He did not want them to miss out on practical ways to make this lifestyle work. Likewise, I hope that as this book comes to an end, you are better equipped for spiritual warfare, using the tools and heavy artillery at your disposal. Remember that this is bigger than you. No matter what you face on earth or in the world, Jesus has already overcome it (John 16:33).

It's time that you acknowledge and activate your Kingdom Identity. You are a son or a daughter of the King, a force to be reckoned with! Stop playing with the devil and wage war on him. No more idle acceptance of wicked things. No more holding unforgiveness in our hearts. No more idol worship. No more being ruled by the flesh over being free in the Spirit. That stops today!

This is war! Pick up your weapons and fight back! You protect yourself with the full armor of God. You fight back with your praise, worship, prayer and intercession, faith, unity, love, and the Sword of the Spirit. You are not a sitting duck. You are a warrior, a soldier, and a heavyweight champ! You are victorious through Jesus Christ!

> *When the people heard the sound of the rams' horns, they shouted as loud as they could. Suddenly, the walls of Jericho collapsed, and the Israelites charged straight into the town and captured it. (Joshua 6:20)*

I blow this spiritual ram's horn, signaling that it is time for the battle to start! It is time to take back the position of authority bestowed upon you by God! Prepare to capture and reclaim every area of your life the devil has infiltrated. Let your war cry be heard from all ends of the earth. Shout as loud as you can, "I DECLARE WAR! I DECLARE WAR! I DECLARE WAR!"

Acknowledgments

Where do I even start? I want to acknowledge God, Jesus, and the Holy Spirit, without whom my life would be dust particles. I tried to get out of writing this book many times, but God would not let me get away from it. I even tried writing other books but would end up with writer's block, or God would give me more ideas for this book instead. I finally conceded and devoted time to writing down what God had given me. It is truly a pleasure and an honor to be used as a vessel of the Lord. I am so glad that He chose me for this assignment!

I acknowledge my mom for being a sounding board and support for me. Thank you for always encouraging me to write. Ever since you realized that I was writing chapter books in kindergarten, you have encouraged me to use this gift of writing. Thank you for not killing a gift before it had time to develop.

I acknowledge my family, who I love seeing and being around. The laughs, the jokes, and the memories we have are irreplaceable. You are irreplaceable. I am grateful for every word of encouragement, mood-uplifting moments, check-in texts or phone calls, and every act of love. Some of you are not even related to me by DNA, but I consider you family because your love and support have been unmatched.

I acknowledge my Eagle Saints Outreach Ministry International family, whom I thank God for regularly. I knew this ministry was unlike any other when I received three correct prophecies during my initial visit! Eagle Saints, you have truly been graced by God to break religious protocol and usher in a Kingdom-driven, Spirit-led culture. May God expand your territory and satisfy every member with long life. May He bless you a thousand times more than you have blessed me.

I thank God for divinely appointed helpers and beta readers. To my spiritual aunt, Alicia, my mother, Reola, and my classmate-turned-friend, Cynthia, I appreciate your openness and honesty in critiquing this manuscript before it went to print. Thank you for willingly accepting this assignment and for your continued support. Though you endured spiritual attacks while assisting me, I am forever grateful for your tenacity and faithfulness to see this project completed. May the favor of God rest richly upon each of you, and may He establish the work of your hands so that you are successful in all that you do (Psalms 90:17).

Lastly, I acknowledge my supporters who are no longer alive to celebrate this moment with me. Though they are not here, I am constantly reminded of the love and support they had for me. In my heart, I know that they would be proud of the person I have become and am still becoming. In loving memory of PawPaw, Dear, Cousin Greg, Justice, and Daddy...

About the Author

 Bree Vanley was born in Arizona but was raised in Arkansas. She began writing at an early age, discovering a love for writing books and poetry before she reached the sixth grade. From a ministry standpoint, she has served in the following capacities: junior and senior usher (total of 15 years), choir ensemble, praise team, Sunday School teacher, and youth leader. Her favorite capacity in which to serve, however, is being a destiny helper. She is a Licensed Professional Counselor and the owner of Heart Matters Therapy, PLLC. She currently resides in the greater Little Rock area, and she enjoys being a big kid, spending time with family and friends, and traveling.

To stay updated about Bree's future projects, visit www.agphouse.com.
General Inquiries can be sent to info@agphouse.com

Thank you for purchasing and reading this book. Please leave a review on Amazon and let me know what you thought.

CHOICE
DESTINATIONS

THE BLUEPRINT SHIFTING LEADING MANAGERS
AND TOP EXECUTIVES FROM
CORPORATE SURVIVING TO
ENTREPRENEURIAL THRIVING

JRAYA
NICOLE

Published by: Fat Elephant
An imprint of Choice Destinations Global LLC

ISBN
Softcover 979-8-218-50627-8
Ebook 979-8-218-50687-2

Library of Congress: 2024918718

Editor: JCB EdPro
Book Designer: Eugene Rijn Saratorio

For more information, please visit:
www.choiceblueprint.com
www.jrayanicole.com

To my mother, Vanessa, whose unwavering belief in my dreams fuels my journey. Thank you for being my anchor and my inspiration.

Dejani and Gabriel, your bright presence and bold steps toward your own destinations light up every path we walk together.

CONTENTS

INTRODUCTION

Welcome to your *Choice Destinations*, a curated space for leading managers and high performing executives to believe, shift, and execute with intentional purpose.

Corporate Surviving to Entrepreneurial Thriving – Tailored for those who feel the pull of starting their own venture, yet they struggle with uncertainty and stagnation. This book provides a strategic blueprint to demystify the path from *Executive to Entrepreneur.*

This book is crafted to guide you toward your freedom of choice in purposeful work and not to debate the merits of a corporate career versus an entrepreneurial endeavor. It's designed to provide a strategic framework—a blueprint—for those considering the significant leap from established corporate roles to the dynamic world of entrepreneurship.

"Why a blueprint?," you may ask.

Think of this blueprint as your comprehensive guide through the complexities of transition. Just as a blueprint in architecture lays out a detailed plan showing how all parts connect and function together, this book serves a similar purpose for your career transition. Without such a plan, moving from a corporate job to entrepreneurship could be haphazard, risky, and unstructured. A well-designed blueprint ensures that you move forward methodically, with every action and decision aligned purposely and effectively towards your desired outcome.

Let's break down a few elements of a typical blueprint and discuss how they relate to the structure of this book:

Title Block: This represents your *identity*. Just as a title block in a blueprint provides essential information about the project, this book helps you redefine and articulate your professional identity as you transition from corporate to entrepreneurial life.

Drawing: Your *vision* for the future. The chapters and sections of this book are drawn to help you visualize your path from where you are now to where you want to be, detailing the steps in between.

Notes: *Reflection and adaptability*. Throughout your journey, there will be annotations—key insights and reflective prompts— that encourage you to think critically and adapt your strategies as circumstances evolve.

Dimensions: *Capacity and resourcefulness.* You'll learn to measure your efforts and the scope of your ambitions accurately, ensuring you leverage your skills and resources effectively

Multiple Views: *Perspectives, pivots, risk tolerance, and resilience.* The book offers various perspectives on the transition process, helping you understand different aspects of the entrepreneurial landscape and sharing strategies to navigate them resiliently.

This well-crafted blueprint ensures you design your choice and approach your intended destinations with clarity, precision, and a strategy customized to your unique strengths and aspirations. Prepare to embark on a journey that is about much more than a career change. It's about transforming how you see yourself in the professional world and seizing the opportunity to drive your success on your own terms. Let's get started on building a future where you thrive, not just survive, in a career that's authentically and rewardingly yours.

PART ONE

ENTITY OF IDENTITY

CHAPTER ONE

You Are?

*Sometimes, you don't know who you are or where you've
been until you have gone through the thing.*

L et us explore the differences of self-perception vs. reality.
As a high performing manager or executive in a corporate
setting, the compounding achievements lend themselves to titles,
money, and influence. You find yourself around people and in
rooms that seem to stamp validity on the American dream. You
developed competitive skills. You have the backing of higher
education, and socially, it looks fantastic and admirable, but then
you go home and feel like you have to take a costume off.

Your authentic self has slowly and silently slipped away behind
the curtain of professional accolades. How does something meant
to be right start to feel wrong? Respectfully, your career track and
the suited aspirations have not been wrong; they have just been
misaligned.

You may feel a sense of guilt that you are even experiencing these inner feelings as you think about your family, friends, and colleagues who witnessed and celebrated you along your journey. Perhaps, you think about the sacrifice and investments of your time and money spent to get to where you are in your career. You tell yourself you are ungrateful for these inner feelings as you hear stories and watch the news of people in impoverished situations and misfortune. You know there are people who would not think twice to be in your shoes. You feel ashamed at the audacity of you thinking something better for you is out there.

Who You Are vs. Who You Think You Are

Who are you? Identity is commonly defined to include gender, race, and age in addition to your socio-environmental experiences regarding family, friends, school, profession, and culture. The byproducts of your identity are your beliefs, morals, thoughts, and attitudes. They represent where the real magic occurs. *Who you think you are* leads the way as your personal compass of self-concept, self-image, and self-esteem. In layman's terms and by definition a compass is a device that indicates direction. It is one of the most important instruments for navigation. The purpose of a compass is to help determine one's heading or orientation, especially when traveling in unfamiliar or off-road locations. With your personal compass, you projected and predicted how your professional career should be.

Your personal compass contains your internal thoughts on your abilities, appearance, self-worth, and respect. The beliefs you hold about yourself and the responses from others are drivers for your professional corporate journey. Whether you arrived at your corporate role with deliberate intention, or your path organically landed on the title you hold, your compass was the catalyst.

I provided for myself as an entrepreneur, specifically as a beauty salon and professional beauty supply owner-operator, for nearly two decades prior to working my way through and up corporate ladders. I do consider myself to have a bit of a hybrid journey; my career path was surface intentional with a very colorful, organic trailblazer path towards a list of successful winning maneuvers that placed me in the likes of the "look momma, I made it!" club. I have a list of 'first to do it' in my family moments. I am a first-generation college graduate. In comparison to my very attentive mother and long absent father, I was the first to own a home in our family. I had thrived many years from the responses I had received from the people I serviced and the people I worked around. Over time, my compass had directed me to obtain higher education as a means to continue to validate myself and appear to be in control. I not only wanted to be great at a craft, but I also wanted to show others that I have the ability to replicate success in the corporate world.

I was running away from the stereotypical mastery and jobs that I saw women have growing up in my low income, black and brown community such as being a hairstylist, having a 'good' government job, or being in small office management. After my many years as a skilled technician, I felt average, low-producing, and unfulfilled. I yearned to be great at something else. My exit strategy from entrepreneurship was forming. In hindsight, my own build up of excitement and expectations about working as a professional in a corporate setting was founded on my perceived lack of status and prominence. To this very day, I love the profession of being a hairstylist. I had just stopped loving myself being in it.

I knew that I needed to continue to bring in a salary that would maintain the lifestyle I had created consistently as an entrepreneur. I also believed that having a college degree was a gateway to unlock doors of opportunities; believe me, it was. My raw and organic beginnings of my path towards corporate success started after I began teaching part-time at a local vocational adult training school as a cosmetology instructor.

A full-time salaried position at that school, seeking an education manager titled Dean of Students, opened up shortly after I started teaching. I was able to outbeat tenured applicants for that position due to the value leadership placed on their education managers having a college degree, combined with relevant technical skills. In just three years, I elevated myself from being a part-time instructor to their Southern Regional School Director of this nationwide career college enterprise. During my tenure, I developed agency approved curricula for cross-state campuses and led my teams to 100% compliance and state accreditations. What I lacked in corporate experience, I more than made up for in real world application and relevance.

You may have or have had expectations of how you would feel, look, and act as a corporate professional. With the help of various streams of media, we have long been provided countless examples of business executives wearing sleek, expensive business attire and using their corporate Amex to purchase business travel to industry exclusive events and locations. The mobility of having a company phone and laptop seemed to be a good trade off if you chose to work from home at your leisure.

When these executives were at the office, they would interact with like-minded ambitious colleagues, have meetings over coffee and treats, enjoy weekly lunches together, and share milestones of individual and organizational achievements. The perks were highly attractive of being attached to a large firm with internal pipelines to profit and prosperity that afforded you and your family a life that would not resemble humble beginnings.

Perhaps you know real life people who held or hold prominent leading corporate roles and highly tout the organization for which they work. From the outside looking and listening in, you envision the same results for your life and career path. Initially, your path can truly be on fire. In fact, it can be euphoric at times. It may not necessarily be a 'cake-walk', but through your capabilities to *respond and be able* (root words for responsible), your affirmations to duplicate a pathway have been proven. With rear views of sacrifice and hyper determination, you now sit in your high-back leather chair and ponder how far you have come, or have you?

The *reality paradox* for many of us is the higher the job title and matched salary for middle managers and high-performance executives, the more minimal we often feel. Your work tasks and project-to-client management are now the star players, not you. Your results get an introduction before your name – the expectations from leadership of being consistently great become heavy. What looks to others as progression has left you at a place of emptiness. You are in the middle of your Cinderella story, and you have yet to find a shoe that fits. Deep down in your gut, you know your current role is not your glass slipper. You are not walking in your true identity. You are misaligned.

In recent times, we are seeing progressive organizations rebuke the standard and vertical pyramid hierarchy organizational chart, opting for wider and flatter structured connectivity amongst the people that work within it. They intentionally prioritized and promoted a collaborative workplace culture that encourages diverse, creative thoughts to grow and scale their corporate visions and missions. This emphasis of collaboration and cross-functional team development has paid off big for the likes of Google, Spotify, and Facebook.

The Slow Drip

When creativity leaks from you as a slow drip, there is a buildup of damage, akin to how an unnoticed and slow leaking pipe can cause considerable damage to a structure; just ask any plumber. It is my belief that you were uniquely made to create as a human being. The ability for you to have impactful inputs is often swallowed by sheer numbers in many large, global corporate organizations. The average number of employees across Fortune 500 U.S. based companies is around 60,815 at the time of writing this book.

I met a woman at a private networking event in the summer of 2021. She sat on a panel with other entrepreneurs, influencers, and speakers and began to discuss her transition from being a high performing corporate professional to the founder of a wildly successful branding and digital marketing agency. A few years prior and before her venture to entrepreneurship, she was driving 90 minutes to work – one way – every single day. She graduated college and landed what she thought to be a dream job at just 20 years old. She went the exact path she was conditioned to take, buying her first home at 22, and by 27 she was making "the big 6 figures." She went on to describe that the corporate path also led her to being exhausted, having limited quality time with her family and friends, and feeling completely unaligned with her purpose.

One night, she began to wrap up details of a very important presentation she had early the next morning. This was a big deal for her career and the company. Her organizational leaders would be present assumingly to watch her close another deal on one of their largest prospective clients to that date. Unfortunately, the deal never made it to the presentation as she fell asleep over her laptop while making final edits in the late hours. She overslept from pure exhaustion. She missed her opportunity to display the results from months of preparation, and when she awoke to multiple texts, calls, and emails, she fell into an immediate mental breakdown, resulting in an extended leave of absence from the company and eventual departure. Her very public miss on the expectation of her was too much for her to handle.

Experiencing the slow drips of polarizing perfectionism and operating outside of your healthy and balanced capacity will eventually reveal itself if it is left unchecked. Because you have chosen to read this book and explore this blueprint to shift from corporate surviving to entrepreneurial thriving, I can confidently state through reflecting, revelating, and rethinking, you are at the crossroad of a professional epiphany. You will experience throughout this book why this is a good place to be.

Beyond Capacity CHECKPOINT

Operating outside of a healthy and balanced capacity in a corporate setting can lead to burnout, stress, and a decline in your overall well-being. Here are signs that you may be operating beyond a healthy capacity:

Consistent Fatigue: Feeling constantly tired, both mentally and physically, regardless of the amount of rest.

Decreased Productivity: A noticeable decline in work performance and productivity, despite putting in long hours.

Increased Irritability: Becoming more easily irritated or frustrated, even in situations that would not typically trigger such reactions.

Cynicism and Negativity: Developing a negative outlook, expressing cynicism about work or colleagues, and a diminished sense of accomplishment.

Difficulty Concentrating: Finding it challenging to focus on tasks and experiencing difficulty concentrating on work assignments.

Health Issues: An increase in physical health issues, such as headaches, muscle tension, and other stress-related symptoms.

Withdrawal from Social Interactions: Withdrawing from social activities or work-related interactions, either physically or emotionally.

Procrastination: Engaging in procrastination or avoidance behaviors, even with tasks that were once manageable.

Poor Sleep Patterns: Disrupted sleep patterns, including difficulty falling asleep, waking up frequently, or experiencing restless sleep.

Lack of Personal Time: Consistently sacrificing personal time, hobbies, and activities outside of work.

CHAPTER TWO

The Unlearn

The sculpture of David is one of the most famous objects in the history of art. This outstanding sculpture was created between 1501 and 1504 by Renaissance genius, Michelangelo. The enormous block of marble used for the statue had lain abandoned for 25 years in the courtyard of the Opera del Duomo because the two artists originally commissioned with the work thought the marble had too many imperfections. Both original artists had abandoned their work after noticing imperfections in the marble's grain. Despite these flaws, Michelangelo took up the monumental challenge of carving the figure. He used the ancient method, "the subtractive process," which is a sculpting technique in which the artist removes material from a larger mass to create the desired form. Let us spend time here focusing on the "chiseling away" of the marble to reveal the figure within.

As in the case of a person having an urgent medical episode that may need CPR as a way to resuscitate life near death, I write this book to provide you with **CPR (clarity, purpose, and resilience)** to remove doubts, rebuke the noise, and revive your personal and professional ambitions to build offense and a defense to what you have been told and conditioned to think negatively about yourself. Here and now is where you stop wandering, leaving things to chance. It is your time to move to take control of your narrative with intention. Let us examine your "Block of Marble."

The process to chisel away things that bear unnecessary weight to our lives can only be had once you have identified what is unnecessary. This process is a sort of a moonwalk, if you will. The late and renowned King of Pop, Michael Jackson's moonwalk dance move captured the imagination of audiences worldwide and became a lasting symbol of his innovative talent and the era's pop culture. Its deceptively simple appearance made it a fun and challenging move for people to try, increasing its popularity. Walking forward is a natural movement, requiring minimal conscious effort, while the moonwalk is a learned skill that demands precise technique, muscle control, and practice to perform smoothly. Forward walking is an instinctive movement that humans learn early in life. I can recall having many good laughs as a child watching people, young and old, attempt the moonwalk to no avail.

Why are we discussing the moonwalk? Because MJ made his signature dance move look easy and effortless, contrary to it being quite challenging to actually do it. The work to address your root identity challenges that led you to career unfulfillment, regret, and fear require deep level examination to the question, "How did I get here?"Walking forward as a top performing professional or leading manager often has you groomed to downplay your feelings of inadequacies and mask emotions to not be seen as weak or incompetent when faced with adversity. The moonwalk to creating a career path that is not only successful, but also deeply fulfilling and aligned with your true self requires self-awareness, intentional action, and ongoing reflection. This unlearning process opens the gate from adversity to advantage.

Your focus on external validations (such as title, salary, or prestige) rather than work and life harmony (intrinsic satisfaction) may have driven your career decisions. Believing that you must fulfill certain roles or achieve specific milestones based on others' expectations (family, society, or professional network) can lead to a misalignment between your career and personal satisfaction. You may not have clearly defined or prioritized your core values, leading to a mismatch between your job responsibilities and the things you find personally meaningful. Your unclear long-term career objectives can result in taking roles that seem advantageous at the moment, but they don't align with your overall aspirations. A fear of stepping outside your comfort zone can lead to staying in a familiar, yet unfulfilling, role instead of seeking opportunities that better match your interests and skills.

I need to be clear at this point. You should not feel guilty for using money as a motivator to explore career and business opportunities. That is a limiting belief that needs to be extinguished right now.

Financial compensation is a form of recognition of the time, skills, and effort invested in work. It reflects the value of your contributions made. Financial stability is essential for meeting basic needs such as housing, food, and healthcare. Without it, pursuing other career or business opportunities may become impractical. Having financial resources provides a sense of security and freedom to explore new opportunities without constant worry about immediate survival. However, using money as a motivator does not negate the value you should place on your journey of peace and purpose.

Leading a manifest of self-sabotaging work behaviors include: feeling internalized perfectionism, overworking for validation, ignoring personal goals, and having a lack of authenticity or suppressing your true self and passions to fit into a corporate mold. A scarcity mindset focused on a lack and competition can make you believe that opportunities are limited, and it is better to stay in a secure, albeit unhappy role. This blueprint designs and builds your space while welcoming the grace needed between your choices and desired destinations. It is paramount to shed those limiting beliefs now to evoke your innermost power that impacts your career-life journey. Your David is soon to be revealed.

Behind the Corporate Curtain

Corporate culture and the higher roles within are filled with high pressure and stress that can lead to beliefs that success must come with significant personal sacrifice, leading to burnout and dissatisfaction. Creativity and innovation are stifled in a lot of these environments. Working in rigid hierarchical corporate structures can create the belief that your potential is capped, and progress is only possible through a slow, linear process. Exposure to toxic work environments, including bullying or discrimination, can cause long-term damage to your self-confidence and belief in your personal worth.

Corporate trauma refers to the psychological and emotional harm that individuals experience due to *prolonged exposure to negative and toxic workplace environments*. The hidden effects of corporate trauma can be far-reaching, impacting both your personal well-being and professional performance. Limited autonomy, negative feedback, unrealistic expectations, harassment and unfair treatment spiral down to frustration, feelings of powerlessness, anxiety, depression, and physical health issues. This can expand outside of you to negatively impact team dynamics and strain personal relationships that often lead to social isolation.

I regularly reflect on my sobering thoughts following my corporate exit as a Senior Business Development Executive for an American Fortune 500 company (ranked number 45 at the time of writing this book). That experience afforded me the expertise to testify to the constant mental renewal that is needed, not only sustain, but to thrive in today's global market. A key takeaway is that the pursuit of a **work-life balance is a fleeting myth**. The reality of work and life is that you will never achieve this "balance." Your professional and personal life will always be interwoven.

My early working years occurred as a young entrepreneur in the beauty industry as an independent operator and a professional beauty supplier and distributor. I like to say that was my incubation stage for the "*business of people.*" During that time, I learned and refined the needed soft skills and high emotional intelligence and responsiveness that would later pave the way for my corporate career success. It is from an entrepreneurial and corporate vantage point that I understand and apply those "people skills." These skills, ranging from communication and empathy to negotiation and conflict resolution, are not just tools; they are essential components that *bridge personal interactions and professional success.* Such capabilities will enhance your ability to lead, inspire, and drive growth within any organizational or business context.

You must know how utterly important it is that your businesses and your roles within align to your personal core values and beliefs. Personal core values and beliefs are closely related concepts that influence behavior and decision-making, but they differ fundamentally in their roles and the ways that they manifest in your life. This is an area we will explore more deeply in chapter 4. The initial work at your crossroad of confusion and fear of the unknown is to unlearn and chisel away negative thoughts and habits to focus on what truly matters, you. Your tide will turn toward the very reason I designed this blueprint for you and professionals alike. **There is more waiting for you.**

A known physics principle is that energy, in various forms, is required to apply forces that change the motion or position of objects. Let's make it simple; "energy moves things." Your capacity to perform at your highest levels consistently requires you to remove the things that do not serve you or your aspirations to make room for what does. You need to redirect that energy for building purposes – literally. Your previous corporate trauma may have planted seeds of mistrust, misplaced competitiveness, and unhealthy comparisons. Your journey to your corporate role may have involved neglecting people who matter in your life, burying things you enjoy, dimming your own light of creativity, or experiencing lackluster and superficial achievements that are short-lived once your numbers of productivity no longer work in your favor from the organizational perspective, or the next fiscal year dawns with new company goals and metrics to match. The energy and efforts to shift to mental spaces and places that serve you, your career, and your purpose are invaluable moving forward.

Risky Intentions

An unlearning technique that will turn adversity to your advantage is *failing forward*. We all make mistakes, and we may have experienced regret. We are human beings. Learning from our failures keeps you moving forward. As you navigate the complexities of your career transition and eye entrepreneurial ventures, embrace failure as an essential stepping stone rather than a setback. Each failure provides invaluable lessons that refine your strategies and strengthen your resolve.

Simply being willing and wishing that your situation will change and be different will never be enough to make the foundational and fundamental changes needed to move the needle of your destined career trajectory. The buildup of adversity you have faced is energy that can be redirected to your *Big Picture*. The energy of time you have spent allowing past events or disappointments to taper down your needed risk tolerance is wasted. Time is a dynamic, limited, and valuable resource that should be utilized effectively and energetically. You must remember taking risks is what led you to your prior successes in life. Being scared to fail is a symptom of the aforementioned root identity challenge – internalized perfectionism. You have to remember as you explore new career opportunities and business ventures that failing is part of the process of pivoting, growing, and thriving. Let us not attempt to fix what is not broken as we move intentionally to future areas of our lives.

Before I entered my first corporate setting, I had informally graduated from the "business school of people." One of the best and freeing decisions of my life was to not go to college directly after high school graduation like many of my peers chose to do. As a recipient of trade education, I chose to be an entrepreneur. I placed value on having autonomy, choosing the people with whom I engaged and avoiding a cap on my income-producing ability. I did not have a blueprint to follow. I was lost in the right direction. I would have never guessed that being in such a creative space prior to my roles in corporate organizations prepared me to have the self-confidence one needs to be a resilient top performer and leading manager. I also learned and mastered the art of pivoting.

The mental capacity and expansion you need to make a strategic shift in your career path will require you to hone your personal pivot power. A pivot can look like not following your parent's footsteps in a specific industry, pursuing work outside the area most closely aligned with your college degree, eyeing entrepreneurship versus remaining a corporate employee, taking lateral promotions to learn a certain skill set, not subscribing to traditional retirement options, and exploring alternate pathways to wealth. The list is infinite. Your timely and deliberate choice to pivot, be nimble, and discern are necessary to adapt to changing market conditions, leverage emerging opportunities, and realign with personal ambition and values. Your future professional relevancy and residency will be spearheaded by the choices you make now to understand that a **comfort zone has always been a danger zone** to the most revered and successful beings on our planet.

The Choice Destinations P7 Blueprint is active and loading to help you build your bridge, turning aspirations to realities. You owe it to your future organizational impacts, entrepreneurship roles, business partners, and ventures to shed the weight of your root identity challenges, embrace calculated risks, and rebuke the noise and remnants of corporate trauma.

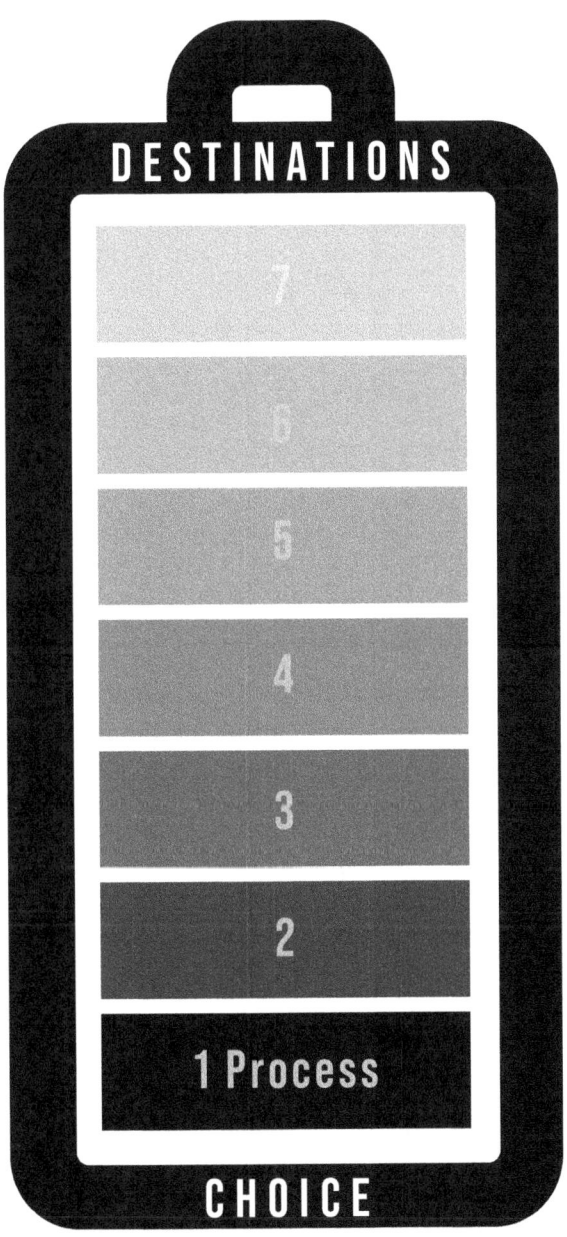

CHAPTER THREE

Desire to Be

"I think, therefore I am" — René Descartes

I AM are two of the most powerful words in the English language. It makes for a simplistic statement, yet it assertively conveys deep personal identity. To have an *audacity of vision* and what you will come to know as *"Big Picture"* thinking later in this book, you should be very cognizant of the words you choose to think and speak that follow your I AM. Your self-reflections at the crossroads of making key decisions in your work and life are of the utmost importance. The famous quote by Descartes, *"I think, therefore I am,"* highlights the importance of self-awareness and consciousness. His quote underscores the idea that the self's realization through thought is the most immediate and palpable experience of your existence. In the design and pouring of your foundations of thoughts that will lead to your innermost satisfaction and faith walk to produce **legacy work**, we now construct your leading steps to your authentic and affirmative I AM declarations.

You have arrived at several destinations throughout your career and life – good and bad. Perhaps a sought-after job promotion did not bring the happiness you thought it would bring. Maybe a company you joined felt like a great match in the beginning, and it ended up having a culture of activities in which you do not wish to participate. No matter what the people, places, and things are, the common factor throughout your journey will always be you. Oftentimes, you will need to be spontaneous and make on-the-spot decisions, especially if you are in leadership. High performing corporate professionals are known for being ambitious and serial goal achievers. However, the measured leaders of the pack all understand that controlling what can be controlled is a gamechanger.

Takeoff...

Interesting moments of my deepest reflections always come for me on an airplane when I am just seated and right before takeoff. During this time, I think about where I'm leaving and where I'm going. I've checked the weather and made the necessary last-minute texts, calls, or emails. Yes, with our modern-day technology, I am aware these tasks can be done during flight. However, since the very beginning of my early travels, I like to dedicate my time spent in the air to my thoughts, whether I have chosen to feed my knowledge appetite with an audiobook or disconnect completely with my most relaxing music playlist. Take note, this in-air relaxation did not come so easily when I first traveled by plane. I used to be so afraid to fly. However, myself and my ability to see a bigger picture as a twenty-something year old entrepreneur predicted business relationships and opportunities that would require global travel. I believed during the idea exploration stages of my business that a geographic expansion of my network was necessary, and as I believed, it came to pass exponentially. My travel plans are now at the forefront of my business planning and opportunities.

It is completely normal when you desire to pivot to a different stage of your career to simultaneously be filled with some levels of doubt. Pushing through that fear will reward you back in the form of met deliverables and goals. You are on your runway of transformation, and you are about to take off.

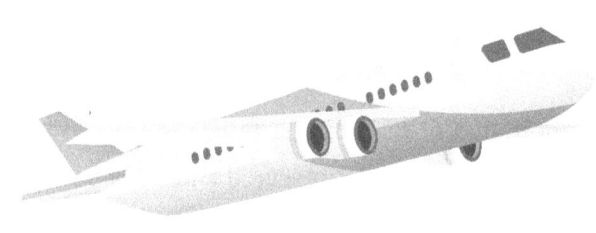

If your next aim and career aspirations have entrepreneurial elements, you must understand that being an entrepreneur is a role inside your business, not the business. This distinction is important as this juncture of separation of identity and entity must remain constant. A business venture can fail, but that does not mean that you are a failure. Remember that we are leaning into the acceptance of *failing forward*. I stand on the belief that work and life is an unbalanced, fluid, and interwoven lifestyle. Walking into a more meaningful purpose of work requires levels of personal identity and self-worth not wholly tied to your business's success or failure. This separation will help you manage stress and decision-making pressure that lie ahead as a trailblazer. Being intentional will make early challenges turn easy because **you were not born to be average** by any means.

We are now seeing a growth of corporate roles governed by entrepreneur spirits in modern organizations. The textbook term is *intrapreneur*, who are individuals within a larger organization who are tasked with developing new projects, products, or initiatives with an entrepreneurial style. Intrapreneurs play a critical role in driving innovation from within an organization. They combine the drive and creativity of an entrepreneur with the resources and stability of an established business, providing a unique blend that can lead to transformative growth and innovation. Intrapreneurship is an effective strategy for organizations looking to stay relevant and competitive in fast-changing industries.

There are countless books, podcasts, info sessions, tv programming, and an abundance of medians of information on the subject of "How to start a business." **This book speaks to the entrepreneur in you – the visionary.** Injustices are served to you when you neglect the self-check needed to make the strategic moves when implementing a pivot or exit strategy from the corporate world. That neglect is comparable to sailing a boat with no wind, having a printer that is out of ink, or starting a construction project without a blueprint to follow. You must create and cultivate the capacity, discipline, and tools to be the needed guide and driving force for your new career direction.

It is vital to grasp that being an entrepreneur involves specific roles and functions within your business environment. This understanding promotes healthier business practices, better personal well-being, and a more sustainable business model that is prepared for growth and adaptation. It is a perspective that can make the difference between a business that is overly dependent on you and one that has the foundation to thrive independently. The tactic to move to a different stage of your work life and towards the place you desire to be is to **become the energy you desire to be around.** Your evolution stage to *become* contains your actions, behaviors, intentions, and thoughts, and they are the foundation for your next and best move.

CEO - Corporate to Entrepreneurship On your terms

Becoming CHECKPOINT

Be a STUDENT: Always stay curious and committed to your learning.
The importance of continuous learning and staying updated with industry trends, new skills, and innovative practice will keep you competitive in an evolving market.

Be an OUTLIER: Dare to be different.
Step outside the norm and explore paths less traveled. Your unique journey can lead to niche markets and unexpected, rewarding destinations.

Be a FORECASTER: Keep your eyes on the horizon.
Anticipate what's coming next in your field and prepare yourself to meet future demands. This foresight is your key to staying ahead, ensuring sustainability and resilience.

Be an ADVOCATE: Champion your causes passionately.
Promote your ideas and defend your values. Your voice is powerful. Use it to shape the world around you.

Be SELFISH: Prioritize your goals, your health, and your growth with balance and boundaries.
Remember, putting yourself first isn't just okay; it's necessary for your success. Self-focus prevents burnout, making a way for you to be a better leader.

Be GRATEFUL: Appreciating what you have enriches your life and deepens your connections.
Recognize the contributions of others and the opportunities that come their way.

Be MINDFUL: Acknowledge your biases and assumptions.
Conduct deep self-assessments to uncover personal biases and assumptions that could negatively affect your decisions and interactions.

Be AWARE: Be on the lookout for networking opportunities and understand the benefits of building a supportive community.
Beware of prioritizing quantity over quality of connections. Focus on cultivating deeper, more meaningful relationships with fewer people rather than collecting contacts.

This process of understanding who you are and unlearning who you are not sets your steps on your new path toward your *Big Picture*. Becoming who you desire to be requires your discernment and structured planning with a hyper ability to block out noise. Noise of comfort, procrastination, distraction, and information overload can derail your progress and desired career design. I cannot downplay the amount of mental focus you will need as you approach this transition in your life.

My final years of being an operator in the beauty industry hit a climax when I met Ms. Lolli. At this juncture of my life was when my reflective thoughts and career optimism were face to face. Ms. Lolli walked in our training room full of beauticians who were then certifying to be state licensed instructors of cosmetology. She introduced herself and shared her long resume of experience in our industry, and then she gave the most intriguing, contrarian statement I needed to move the needle of planning my career exit and elevation strategy. She simply said, "Who wants to be a 60-year-old hairstylist?" It was a defining moment in terms of valuing the way I spent my time and the type of energy I wished to commit to make a living. I became a "work smarter, not harder" advocate from that point on.

You see, Ms. Lolli's message was not intended to demean the efforts of aging practitioners working in the beauty industry. She was painting a picture with her words to provoke a move towards a more thought leadership role versus being an operator of the industry – less muscle and more mental. Ms. Lolli understood that physically demanding jobs over time had more limits than contributions as an educator. Thus, my shift to corporate life began with an abundant entrepreneurial spirit advantage and momentum to lead the way.

PART TWO

RECOGNIZE YOUR CORE

CHAPTER FOUR

Safekeeping

I magine your core values and beliefs as treasures locked within a personal vault. This vault is not just any safe; it contains the essence of who you are and what you stand for—the principles you rely on when faced with critical decisions about your career. As you consider a pivot from an unsatisfactory job or leap towards entrepreneurship, it is this vault that you will turn to, ensuring that your next steps are not only strategic but also true to your deepest convictions. This chapter will help you articulate and reinforce your personal values, so when the time comes for you to choose to pivot, you do so with a clear sense of direction and purpose. You will appreciate why these values are not just abstract concepts but practical tools that shape and define the very trajectory of your professional lifestyle.

Let's explore what it means to unlock your personal vault. We will delve into the importance of recognizing and understanding your core values – those elements that are non-negotiable and defining for you. These values serve as your personal compass, guiding you through the uncertainties of career transition and helping you navigate towards roles and opportunities that align with your authentic self. The journey to entrepreneurship or any new career path is paved with challenges and opportunities. Like the intricate mechanisms of a vault, understanding your values helps decode these challenges, turning potential obstacles into stepping stones towards success. Whether it is the courage to innovate, the resilience to persevere, or the integrity to lead with compassion, your personal core values are key to unlocking a fulfilling and successful career.

Creating a scalable business while working *in purpose, on purpose,* and *with purpose* happens when the work is aligned to your vault of values. Your core belief system is locked in. Beliefs and values often work in tandem, with **beliefs shaping how we see the world and values guiding our actions within it**.

For example, if someone believes that businesses have a responsibility to their communities, that is a belief. The resulting high value would be placed on corporate social responsibility. Beliefs frame the world in which they operate, while values dictate how they navigate this world. Effective career decisions, especially those driven by a desire to achieve meaningful work, require a deep understanding and alignment of both beliefs and values. Here's a corporate case scenario that underscores actions based on core beliefs.

Shattering the Glass Ceiling: One Woman's Advocacy for Diversity in Finance

Consider a professional woman in a traditionally male-dominated industry such as finance. Despite her qualifications and achievements, she encounters the "glass ceiling," a metaphor for the invisible barriers that prevent women from advancing to the highest levels in their organizations. She *believes* that gender equality is crucial for the health and success of any organization. She holds a strong conviction that diverse leadership brings varied perspectives that can drive innovation and improve decision-making processes. She *values* fairness, transparency, and equal opportunity. These values are central to her professional identity, and they guide her interactions and career choices. Through advocacy, she made the decision to become more vocal about the lack of gender diversity in leadership roles within her company. She believes that by speaking up, she can influence change, not just for herself but for other women in her organization.

Her **Strategic Actions** included:

Internal Initiatives: She proposes the creation of a diversity and inclusion committee at her company and volunteers to lead it. She works on initiatives that aim to dismantle the glass ceiling such as mentorship programs for women and diversity training workshops.

Policy Advocacy: She collaborates with HR to review and revise promotion policies to ensure they are transparent and fair, advocating for criteria that mitigate unconscious bias.

Networking: She joins professional alliances for women in tech, seeking mentorship from other women who have navigated similar challenges and can provide guidance and support.

You can unlock more by ...

Engage in Visibility Projects: Get involved in projects that boost visibility for underrepresented groups within your company. Showcasing diverse contributions can inspire others and highlight the value of inclusivity.

Develop Personalized Plans: Encourage your leadership to support personalized development plans that align your personal career goals with the company's diversity objectives.

This case scenario serves as a powerful example of how one individual, empowered by their values and initiative, can affect meaningful change within an organization with an entrepreneurial mindset. You can enhance your career to be more meaningful when your actions are aligned to your personal vault. The scenario illustrates the impact of applying the principles you believe in and intentionally working to make them a reality in your professional environment.

Unlocking your vault is about tapping into the deep reservoir of your personal beliefs and values that steer your professional journey. Standing at a crossroad of your life, you can utilize your beliefs to propel yourself and your lifestyle forward. When you evoke your entrepreneurial spirit within a corporation, you transform your work environment not just for yourself, **but** for others around you. The manifestations from your vault take shape and transform into leadership, influence, and contribution. **Becoming a true agent of change and controlling your narrative can start with:**

- **Continual Learning & Skill Development**
- **Joining Networks & Seeking Mentorship**
- **Spearheading Initiatives**
- **Build Your Personal Branding**

It's not just about climbing the corporate ladder; it's about ensuring the ladder is up against the right wall.

Your commitment to your values can lead to profound changes in your organization and immense personal satisfaction, knowing you are not only advancing your career, but you are also paving the way for future generations in your authentic authority. Therefore, lean into what you hold true and let your beliefs and values light up your path to your success. Your future destinations depend on the choices you make today.

— Take a moment to consider your personal beliefs with the resulting values

I Believe _____

Therefore I Value:

1. _____
2. _____
3. _____

Your Personal Vault

Protecting Your Vault

At this point, you are able to recognize and understand your belief-to-value system. Your real pieces to peace and purpose involve creating and maintaining environments that foster and safeguard your personal and professional growth. The legacy of work you leave in your professional lives is fully dependent on the boundaries you set now. Placing value on you and your abilities is not an act of *corporate treason* – another one of those limiting beliefs.

You are not any form of a traitor, and you are not guilty of corporate treason when you value yourself and the things that serve you. Knowledge is void without application. My own personal vault is built with my beliefs in the Biblical concepts of faith and resilience. Allow me to share with you a principle found in the Bible that emphasizes the importance of putting knowledge into practice. In the Christian Bible, James 1:22-25 (NIV) underscores this concept:

> *Do not merely listen to the word, and so deceive yourselves. Do what it says. Anyone who listens to the word but does not do what it says is like someone who looks at his face in a mirror and, after looking at himself, goes away and immediately forgets what he looks like. But whoever looks intently into the perfect law that gives freedom, and continues in it—not forgetting what they have heard, but doing it—they will be blessed in what they do.*

This Biblical passage is a clear call for believers to act on their knowledge and faith, not just to hear or understand it. The implication is that knowledge or faith without action is incomplete and ineffective. This idea is a central theme in many Biblical teachings in which understanding is meant to lead to transformation and action.

You may encounter headwinds that cause you to think that putting yourself first is an act of betrayal. In those moments, you have agreed that you owe an organization a very valuable thing – your future. **Your allegiance to an organization should never be higher than the dedication applied to yourself.** It is well proven that a company will replace you, your role, and your responsibilities upon your exit to continue on to their corporate missions. This is where you keenly activate your *"audacity of vision"* or the willingness to be bold and affirmative on what you believe at present is best for your future self. While doing so, a hedge of protection must be ever-present on your path to purpose. Here's a few ways to strengthen your internal foundation, helping you to navigate choices with greater clarity and assurance:

- **Practice Mindful Reflection**: Allocate time each day for reflective journaling to align your daily actions with your core values.
- **Set Clear Personal Boundaries**: Identify and communicate what you are willing to accept in both your personal and professional life and what you are not. This will safeguard your mental energy and keep your focus sharp.

- **Build a Support Network:** Cultivate a circle of supportive people who reinforce your values and support your decisions.

- **Engage in Strategic Unplugging**: Schedule digital detoxes and regularly unplug from digital devices to clear your mind and prevent information overload. Use this time to reconnect with your thoughts and priorities without external influence.

- **Maintain Physical Wellness:** Engage in regular exercise. Eat balanced meals and ensure adequate rest to enhance mental clarity and decision-making.

One of my favorite and best-selling authors, Robin Sharma, often writes on the concept of safeguarding your personal and professional environments to optimize your performance, growth, and well-being. In his impactful book, *The Everyday Hero Manifesto*, Sharma introduces the transformative concept of "protecting your ecosystem" in your work and personal life. He eloquently argues that fostering a supportive personal and professional environment is essential for sustainable success. As we delve into strategies to enhance your career path, the ideas presented serve as a vital resource and encourage us to nurture and protect a balanced life in which personal well-being and professional ambitions are in harmony.

Contrary to the nurturing aspects of an ecosystem, an *egosystem* is driven by self-centered, short-sighted desires that prioritize personal gain at the expense of a person's broader well-being. This often leads to toxic work environments, strained relationships, and unsustainable lifestyle choices that can ultimately be detrimental to personal growth and happiness. I am here to introduce and to stretch your mind and awareness to lasting, foundational, and critical decision making versus what is temporary, seasonal, and popular. Let us take note of the difference:

Eco vs. Ego System CHECKPOINT

Aspect	ECO (Nurturing)	EGO (Self-Serving)
Self-Awareness	Engage in regular self-reflection and mindfulness practices.	Ignore internal reflections; act impulsively based on desires and conveniences.
Relationships	Build deep, meaningful connections; focus on reciprocity.	Prioritize superficial connections that enhance status or personal gain.
Leadership	Lead with empathy; prioritize team success and collaborative achievements.	Focus on personal accolades and dominance over others.
Learning	Commit to lifelong learning; openly seek and apply feedback for improvement.	Dismiss feedback and new learning opportunities; rely on past successes.
Gratitude	Practice daily gratitude; acknowledge the contributions of others.	Overlook the role of others in successes; focus on self-promotion.
Work-Life Balance	Strive for harmony between work and personal life; prioritize health.	Sacrifice health and relationships for career advancement or financial gain.
Humility	Recognize and admit limitations; see failures as learning opportunities.	Defend actions and decisions, denying limitations or faults.

It is crucial to recognize that navigating your life-changing choices strategically is profoundly influenced by a deep exploration and understanding of your authentic self. By unveiling the core aspects of who you are, you set a solid foundation and establish clear expectations for a path that is not only rewarding **but** uniquely yours. Your *logistics of purpose* contain your leading steps necessary to gracefully exit situations that no longer serve you and allow you to step confidently toward new opportunities. You are not merely leaving one phase behind. You are proactively moving towards a purpose-driven future, equipped with the knowledge and strategies to navigate your career and life with intention and mastery.

It is wise to add to your personal vault the mantra, "**You don't get what you deserve; you get what you negotiate,**" as we move on to examine and construct the making of a Beautiful Exit. Your journey, while deeply personal, is also universally relevant as each step you take enriches your understanding of yourself and enhances your ability to make informed, impactful decisions.

CHAPTER FIVE

Mr. Wind

"What lies behind us and what lies before us are tiny
matters compared to what lies within us."
– Ralph Waldo Emerson

W ho would have thought that three simple household items would make way for a show stopping performance. The start of my third-grade year was on the heels of a family move from a military base in Heidelberg, Germany to Ft. Sam Houston in San Antonio, TX. Our new location, my new school, and new faces and friends required an adjustment, prepping my life ahead to expect and accept change. It was a great lesson at a young age! Some of my memories have become blurry over time, and some are standout, unforgettable life moments that have become my relied upon, good place to revisit as a reminder of how courageous I can be.

You Are Enough

At my new school, I had a role in a school play, and my character's name was Mr. Wind. I don't quite remember my classmates' character names, but I am pretty sure it was along the lines of Ms. Sunshine and Mr. Rain; you get the point. In preparation for this role, I was supposed to memorize my lines and be responsible for my costume. Although I have no recollection of the lines I spoke in the play, I vividly remember how my mother and I prepared my onstage wardrobe. She knew my character, and she knew that I wished to be big, bold, and loud like a gust of wind could be. She gathered three things: an oversized white t-shirt, a black permanent marker, and a pillow. We then drew a big cumulus-shaped cloud on the front of the shirt with puckered lips that was blowing a force of air. When I put that shirt on, we stuffed it with the pillow to further add to the robust appearance of a cloud that would likely be present on windy days. Let me just say that I absolutely rocked my performance as Mr. Wind.

The way I showed up in that makeshift costume you would have thought I was to perform in a Broadway show that day. Memorizing my lines, turning vision to reality with my costume, and having the backing of my mother was all I needed to have the boost of self-confidence to show up in a new school amongst new peers with that level of courage. That t-shirt, pillow, and marker were what we had around the house, and we made it work. It is a gentle reminder of the good ole saying, "Use what you got to get to where you want."

My starring role as Mr. Wind

Imagine someone with a background in education who wants to transition their career to business consulting. By "using what they got," they might leverage their expertise in educational structures to offer specialized consulting services to educational institutions or edtech startups, thus entering the business world through a familiar sector. In essence, "using what you got to get to where you want" is about being empowered and taking proactive steps to shape your journey. It encourages you to not wait for the perfect moment or abundance of resources, but instead, you should creatively use whatever you have right now to advance toward your goals.

You may have degrees, certifications, specialized training, and a list of accolades to match. You may even be adding to your credentialing as you read this book. However, when approaching uncertainty in new environments, you have to know that you and your uniqueness are not to be shrunk. It is in the application of you and your abilities that you win. When choosing to enter a new venture or new industry or when you decide to change your career interest, YOU ARE ENOUGH. When choosing yourself over a toxic work environment that likely is more damaging than any change you could make there, YOU ARE ENOUGH. Resources during your journey may be limited, or they may be abundant at different stages of your career. The repeating theme throughout your journey should be to **bet and believe in yourself.**

While we strive to innovate and evolve, it's equally important to recognize the aspects of our strategies and processes that are already effective. Moving forward doesn't always mean overhauling everything; sometimes, it's about building on the strong foundations we already have. By maintaining what works and only adjusting what needs improvement, we can ensure that our energy and resources are directed most efficiently towards sustainable growth and success.

—Take a moment to reflect on a time when your courage to act in the unknown led to a successful outcome. Consider how it has equipped you for critical decision-making.

In the previous chapter, we discussed the vital safekeeping of your personal vault. Equally as important, you must also know that bits of vulnerabilities must occur for the sake of your forward motion. I am here to attest to you how your accumulated experiences of adverse events in your professional and private life will empower you to say yes to opportunity and no to distraction and potential sources of unfulfillment. You will know how to place quantifiable, proven value on your abilities to ensure your trade-off for your creative, innovative work contributions are financially rewarded and validated. Perfectionism and comparison tend to resurface in the moments when a decision must be made at a pivotal crossroad of your career. It is through your vulnerability lens that you focus on your *Big Picture* and realize that staying in your current role will be exponentially regretful over choosing your own career terms. The consequence of inaction or misguided action is accepting the status quo. **You were not born to be average.**

Vulnerability is not a weakness. It is a valuable emotional tool for self-reflection and decision-making. By acknowledging your true feelings about past offenses in your current role, including the byproducts of fear of change or failure, you open yourself to more profound insights about what you truly want from your career. Vulnerability brings about emotional honesty and challenges you to think about where you want to be in the future and whether your current path will lead you there. Long-term consequences of remaining in a role that doesn't align to you or your purpose lead to a waste of your limited time here on Earth, your efforts, and your energy – the energy you need every bit of to get you where and what you desire to be.

Your good and bad experiences in the workplace contribute to your personal and professional growth, allowing a more introspective approach and creating emotional awareness. **Your Corporate Currency is the sum of all your experiences within the corporate world—the people you've met, the processes you've mastered, and the politics you've navigated.** This currency isn't just about what you've done, but it is about how what you've done has shaped who you are. This brings me to a good place to explain the quote, "You don't get what you want; you get what you negotiate." Keep in mind that your goal should be to work smarter, not harder.

Set Your Terms

In order to navigate career transitions confidently, you will need to be a good negotiator. **You must internally (know) and externally (show) your advocacy for yourself.** Every challenge you've faced in the corporate world has added to your *Corporate Currency*, making you more resilient and adaptable. As a corporate professional, negotiating your worth comes in the forms of not just salary, but your role and responsibilities. As an entrepreneur, the financial fruit of negotiation power can look like:

- **Equity and Ownership** - determine your share of future profits and your level of control in the business.

- **Partnerships and Alliances** - negotiating roles, responsibilities, and benefits is key to ensuring that the partnership is mutually beneficial and aligns with strategic goals.
- **Favorable Client and Contract Terms** - pricing, payment schedules, and deliverables directly impact your revenue and cash flow.
- **Supplier and Vendor Deals** - reduce costs and improve profit margins.
- **Intellectual Property Rights** - can significantly impact your business's profitability and growth.

As an entrepreneur and visionary for your business, negotiating your worth extends beyond your salary and encompasses every aspect of your business operations – from startup to exit. Negotiation is an art that requires understanding your worth and being able to articulate it confidently; these are skills that you have fine-tuned through your corporate experiences. Simply being deserving is not enough. Have you ever seen a colleague receive a promotion, and you know they were not the most qualified person to get that new role and the benefits that come with it? You knew of at least 3 other colleagues who were interested in the advancement who would have been a better fit. What you may not have witnessed was that candidate's intentional politics behind the scene — the casual watercooler gestures and drive-by coffee breaks by the lead manager's office, the Saturdays on the golf course with decision makers, and emails of thanks to the busiest of bees at the office who will rave about them whenever a chance is given. That candidate's social maneuvers outweighed the other competing colleagues' qualifications. Yes, that is a degree of negotiation.

Your insight, valuation, and ability to articulate your *Corporate Currency* will help you pivot from a position of strength as you consider making significant changes to your career path. This section of your journey involves recognizing how your experiences equip you to handle future uncertainties. For instance, navigating a company merger may have tested your adaptability, but it also taught you invaluable lessons about managing change; your learned lessons that can help you thrive in dynamic entrepreneurial environments. You may feel forced to remain in a certain industry, role, or location because of the familiarities you have and the time you invested. Have the following myths plagued your thoughts?

Conquering Myths:

- **Traditional Learning Models** - Traditional educational models that emphasize routine learning and conformity over creativity and innovation can stifle confidence in one's ability to think outside the box.
- **Niche Focus** - Specialized education and training in a particular field can create a belief that one's skills are not transferable to other industries or roles.
- **Golden Handcuffs** - The idea that high compensation, benefits, or perks in a current role are too valuable to give

up, even if the job is unsatisfying or doesn't align with one's personal or professional growth goals.

Leveraging Your Corporate Currency for a Beautiful Exit

This chapter's focus on equipping you with the confidence, readiness, and clarity needed to make a pivotal career change gives you leverage in global markets. While financial planners and strategists are invaluable for mapping out the details of your safety nets and money plans, my focus here is on preparing you emotionally and strategically for your exit. Later in this book, I will be sure to hand off tried and tested *moves that matter* as you transition into a fulfilling new chapter, whether you are functioning as an entrepreneur or operating in another capacity.

At the time of writing this book, generally, about 20% of new businesses fail during the first two years of being open, 45% fail during the first five years, and 65% fail during the first ten years. Only 25% of new businesses make it to 15 years or more. One of the most commonly cited reasons for these failures is a lack of preparedness, which includes poor business planning, inadequate financial management, and insufficient understanding of the market. A *Beautiful Exit* isn't just about leaving a job; it's about transitioning with purpose, readiness to face risks, and the adaptability to navigate the unforeseen. It's about using your accumulated *Corporate Currency* and emotional intelligence to forge a path that aligns with your deepest aspirations. As a leading manager or top-performing executive, you already possess a rich set of skills. Let's look at how a few of these can serve as your *keys* to unlocking new doors of opportunity on your entrepreneurial journey:

- **Project Management:** Bring your knack for overseeing projects from start to finish to ensure future ventures run just as smoothly.
- **Networking:** Tap into your network to unlock new opportunities and forge strategic partnerships.
- **Strategic Forecasting:** Use your sharp forecasting skills to stay ahead of market trends and set up your venture for success.
- **Data Analysis:** Make smart, data-driven decisions to steer your business strategy and growth.
- **Compliance Oversight:** Keep your new venture on the right side of industry regulations with your compliance know-how.
- **Customer Centricity:** Put your customer-first approach to work to boost satisfaction and cultivate a loyal following.
- **Risk Management:** Apply your skills in identifying and managing risks to smoothly navigate the ups and downs of entrepreneurship.
- **Adaptability:** Leverage your ability to adapt to changing situations—an essential skill as you dive into the entrepreneurial world.

Combining your work and educational background with your rich *Corporate Currency* and these essential *skill keys* equips you with a formidable toolkit. Remember, YOU ARE ENOUGH. Your new deep-seated belief coupled with your skills and experience is the wind that will fill the sails of your new venture, propelling you to new heights of resilience and achievement. It is the very essence of moving like a **CEO - Corporate to Entrepreneurship On your terms.** Embrace this journey with the confidence that you are not just moving on; you are moving up and operating in alignment with your true purpose.

CHAPTER SIX

But Why?

W elcome to a vital stage in your journey of self-discovery and career advancement—understanding the 'Why' behind your decisions. Lacking a clear 'Why' as an entrepreneur places you at a deficit and increases your likelihood of faltering when challenges arise. You just read the statistics that nearly half of new businesses fail within 5 years of their launch. Which is why you, the visionary, entrepreneur, CEO, advisor, and navigator, must be ready to operate with clarity and be constantly reminded of the purposes you seek to serve. Let's dig into how identifying and embracing your deepest motivations can transform your approach and sustain your progress.

Knowing your 'Why' is more than just a motivational phrase; it is to be a pillar of your career choice and your accountability tool. Here's why it matters:

- **Mental Leverage for Non-Negotiables**: Your 'Why' *solidifies* the boundaries that align to your core values, ensuring that your career moves don't compromise what's most important to you.

- **Unveiling Purpose and Intentions**: A clear 'Why' *reveals* the deeper intentions behind your career moves, providing a beacon that guides your journey.

- **Discerning and Eliminating Distractions**: With a *well-defined* 'Why', you can easily spot and eliminate distractions that veer you off your desired path, reducing the likelihood of diverging into less meaningful ventures.

Here's an example of a 'Why' statement from a corporate executive who desires a career change that will provide greater control over their career path and enhance their personal life:

"My purpose is to fully leverage my extensive leadership skills and business acumen to craft a career that not only challenges and fulfills me professionally but also respects and enhances my personal life. I am committed to creating more autonomy in my work, enabling me to innovate, make impactful decisions, and lead on my terms. This shift is driven by my deep belief in the value of work-life harmony, where success is measured not just by achievements within the office but also by the quality of life outside of it. My goal is to redefine success on my own terms, ensuring that my professional endeavors allow for substantial personal growth and time for my passions and relationships, thereby cultivating a life that is as rewarding personally as it is professionally."

This statement underscores motivations for seeking change, greater autonomy, a healthier personal well-being, and a grander idea of what success really means to them.

Your source of resilience and energy renewal when your motivation may be low is right here in the 'Why'. It rekindles your drive and passion during your journey. As an entrepreneur, you must build your muscle by *"benchmarking your own success."* The traditional corporate expressions of promotion, bonuses, and perks for being a top performing professional are no longer there to validate your merits. You must be the creator and analyzer of your new measurables. Directly linking your goals to your motivations and 'Why' will result in an easier, smarter way to assess your progress, celebrate milestones, and recalibrate strategies as necessary. This is exactly how you activate and shift your mindset towards being a –

CEO - Corporate to Entrepreneurship On your terms

— Take a moment here to create your 'Why'

Consider answering a few of these questions:

1. Why is change needed right now?
2. What inspires you in your career and personal life?
3. What impact do you want to make?
4. How does success look to you?
5. What kind of work environment makes you thrive?
6. What are you not willing to compromise on?
7. How does work-life harmony look?

Janice Bryant-Howroyd, one of the first African American women to own and operate a billion-dollar company, is a prominent entrepreneur and businesswoman, and she once said:

> *"One of the most powerful forces in your entrepreneurial journey is your belief in yourself. Trust your instincts, have faith in your capabilities, and don't let anyone else's doubts or limitations define what's possible for you."*

This powerful affirmation underlines the importance of self-trust, which is supported by a firm understanding of your 'Why.'

Janice Bryant-Howroyd's monumental success can be attributed to a clear set of 'Why's' that have consistently guided her entrepreneurial journey and her firm belief in her mission. These 'Why's' not only defined her approach to business, but they also kept her focused on making impactful contributions to society and the business world. She is not only a successful entrepreneur, but she is also an advocate for education and workforce development. She is known for speaking on the importance of diversity in business and the workforce. One of her 'Why' statements is based on growing up in the segregated South where she experienced and understood the value of diversity and inclusion firsthand. She was driven to ensure that everyone had equal opportunities to thrive, regardless of their background. She is also a firm believer in the power of education and lifelong learning as tools for personal and professional growth. By adhering closely to her 'Why's', Janice Bryant-Howroyd has not only built a highly successful business, but she has also crafted a legacy of positive impact on society, serving as a role model for ethical leadership and the power of staying true to one's beliefs and values.

When your career decisions are backed by a clear 'Why', transitions become opportunities rather than obstacles. Being passionate about your 'Why' helps you break free from the comfort zones and golden handcuffs that hold you back, empowering you to seek opportunities that fulfill you deeper. Knowing your 'Why' equips you with the clarity and confidence needed to make decisions that aren't just reactive, but proactive and transformative. For most, this is not an automatic revelation and process. You must enter a contract with yourself, a binding agreement to value yourself. I encourage you to form a **Personal Capability Statement.**

When we break down the word "capability," we're left with two powerful concepts: "capable" and "ability." These words are foundational to understanding what you can achieve both personally and professionally.

Capable implies having the power and competence to accomplish tasks or face challenges effectively. *It's about your potential and possibility—recognizing that you have the inherent qualities needed to succeed.* This term empowers you, reinforcing the idea that you are equipped to handle what comes your way. [Your *Corporate Currency*]

Ability, on the other hand, focuses on the skills you've cultivated and the actions you can perform. It's more about proven competence—*what you have demonstrated you can do through your actions.* This term is practical and grounded in your experiences and acquired knowledge. [Your *Skills Keys*]

Know The Difference – Both the 'Why' and the Personal Capability Statement are foundational tools in your personal and career development, but they serve distinct roles in guiding your professional journey.

The 'Why' refers to your underlying motivations and core reasons that drive your professional decisions and behaviors. It essentially answers the question, "Why do I do what I do?"

This statement is deeply rooted in your values, passions, and long-term aspirations.

vs.

The Personal Capability Statement, on the other hand, is a comprehensive outline that not only declares your 'Why,' but it also shares your specific skills, strengths, goals, and the commitments you make to yourself and your career. It serves as both a declaration and a roadmap.

**The 'Why' serves as a central guiding principle.
The Personal Capability Statement functions as a
comprehensive plan.**

The very essence of your aspirations and intentions needs to be outlined in your Personal Capability Statement. Your 'Why' should be the driver in your statement to keep you accountable and set your purpose. This agreement with yourself will act as your *decision filter, helping* you to decide whether your potential actions and opportunities align with your fundamental purpose. Your 'Why' allows you to perform regular reflective practices that invite you to consider how you have lived up to your statement and what adjustments are needed to make alignment with your aspirations. Your 'Why' will steer your professional reputation based on authenticity and reliability, which can open doors to more aligned opportunities and collaborations. Your 'Why' can reduce your internal conflicts and enhance your overall well-being by ensuring your actions are consistent with your values.

Your 'Why' will give you depth and meaning to your professional pursuits. The Personal Capability Statement will provide you with the structure necessary to realize those pursuits. By adding your 'Why' into your Personal Capability Statement, you essentially forge a personal contract that doesn't just guide your career; it becomes a compass for your overall fulfillment and integrity. Think of this as a living testament to what you stand for and where you want to go. It will guide you through your professional journey with clarity and intention, holding you accountable not just to professional goals but to living a life that's deeply aligned with your values and purpose. Therefore, keep it close. Reflect on it often and let it steer you confidently toward the future you envision for yourself – your *Big Picture*.

Making Your Statement

To make the most out of your Personal Capability Statement, consider the following tips:

- **Review Regularly:** Keep your statement visible in your work spaces or save it in an accessible place. Regular reflection on your statement helps ensure your actions remain aligned with your goals.

- **Update as Necessary:** As you grow and evolve, so should your statement. It's a living document meant to adapt alongside your changing aspirations and capabilities.
- **Share When Appropriate:** Utilize your statement in professional settings or platforms (such as LinkedIn) to concisely and powerfully articulate your professional spirit and ambitions.

Get your downloadable Personal Capability Statement fillable form at choiceblueprint.com

Pursuing and embracing a peaceful journey is subjective because your pathway to it will look different from others. Your *pillars of peace* serve as a foundation to help you outline your transition out of the corporate world. Your ability to articulate your 'why' – the core reason that drives all your career decisions – is critical as it details your personal and unique capabilities.

Pillars of PEACE

Plan Your Beautiful Exit

- **Takeaway**: You're contemplating a career transition; planning is your best friend. A well-thought-out exit can be the start of an exciting new chapter.
- **Action**: Start sketching out your Beautiful Exit plan. What are the key steps? Who can help you? Begin to put the pieces together.

Expand Your Skill Keys

- **Takeaway**: The skills you don't yet have can be the gateway to new opportunities. Don't limit yourself to familiar territories.
- **Action**: Choose one skill you've always wanted to develop and commit to starting a course or training program this month. Growth happens outside your comfort zone.

Assess Your Corporate Currency

- **Takeaway**: Remember, your unique experiences and skills are your currency in the corporate world. Reflect on what you've learned so far.
- **Action**: List out your top three professional experiences that define your journey. How have these shaped your approach to work? Use this insight to steer your future decisions.

Commit to Continuous Learning

- **Takeaway**: The most successful professionals are lifelong learners. There's always something new to discover.
- **Action**: Identify one area relevant to your career where you feel you could learn more. Find a book, a workshop, or a seminar that can deepen your understanding in that area.

Embrace Change and Adaptability

- **Takeaway**: Change is inevitable, especially in today's fast-paced world. Adapting swiftly and effectively sets you apart.
- **Action**: Reflect on a recent change in your life or career. How did you handle it? Next time, challenge yourself to respond even more proactively.

You are doing the work, investing your time in *defining your true self and understanding your value and your 'Why'*...Congratulations on taking charge!

We move on to build on the clarity gained here by exploring how to strategically implement your plans.

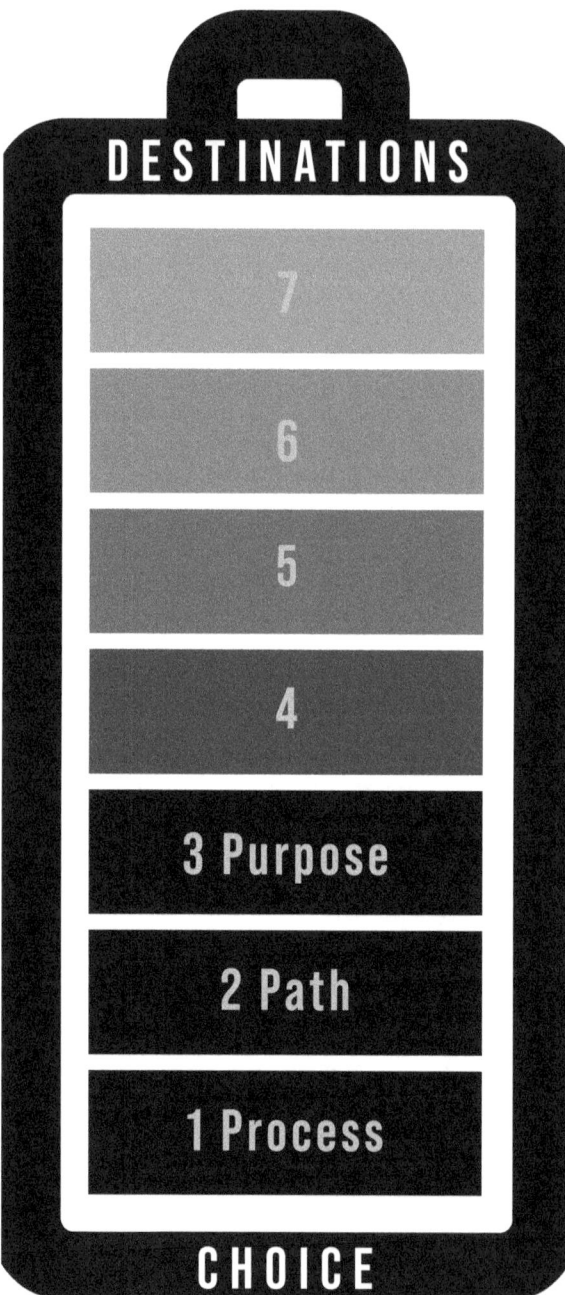

DESTINATIONS

7

6

5

4

3 Purpose

2 Path

1 Process

CHOICE

PART THREE

CULTIVATE VISIONARY POWER

CHAPTER SEVEN

Moves that Matter

"Before the mind can work efficiently, we must develop
our perception of the outcomes we expect to reach."
– Maxwell Maltz

The understanding of your true identity and purpose calls for applying the knowledge you have that will serve them both. The actions suggest the literal meaning of the catchphrase, "Put your money where your mouth is." I believe it is better to say, "Put your money where your mind is." This is exactly why it is counterproductive to compare your journey to other people's journeys. Comparison can distract and disrupt your path. This deeper level of planning is about applying strategies that are uniquely suited to your goals and your circumstances. This requires a deliberate alignment and design of tailored steps. Your intentional moves forward are your *logistics of purpose.*

logistics: *noun*

1. The detailed organization and implementation of a complex operation, often involving the planning and management of the flow of information, resources, and personnel needed to achieve specific objectives efficiently.
2. The art and science of managing and controlling the flow of goods, energy, information, and other resources like products, services, and people, from the source of production to the marketplace.
3. The handling of the details of an operation, which includes the organization, planning, and execution necessary to achieve desired outcomes effectively and efficiently.

Logistics of Purpose is your strategic orchestration of actions, resources, and intentions to align every step of your work-life journey with your core personal and professional objectives.

Here is where you choose to no longer shrink in zones of comfort and move to stretch yourself to new heights. You are expanding and controlling what you can, while accepting realities of luck, fate, or the outcome of your own might along the way. Maximizing your *logistics of purpose* to create the most optimal opportunities starts with your ability to *reverse engineer*. The process of reverse engineering is starting with the end in mind. **Big Picture** thinking cannot exist without having your intended arrival points at the forefront.

Audacity of Vision

I have casually mentioned "Big Picture" thinking throughout this book, but a more formal introduction is needed. The Big Picture concept is not just having a goal or a target. It is your ultimate vision for your career and life, encompassing your highest aspirations and deepest values. *The Big Picture should serve as your guiding star that influences your most prominent decisions, ensuring each step is not only intentional but also meaningful.*

The Big Picture is essentially your overarching vision for your life and career. It is more than just a specific milestone; it is a comprehensive image of what you aspire to achieve across different aspects of your life. This could include your desired professional achievements, the kind of lifestyle you want to maintain, the relationships you wish to cultivate, and the personal growth you aim to attain.

The Big Picture represents your *audacity of vision* – a bold, clear idea of where you want your professional life and personal achievements to align. It's about knowing, not only where you're going but also why you're headed there. This vision is fueled by your understanding of who you truly are and, equally important, who you are not. It is a destination shaped by your authentic self and your core values, refined through your experiences and the challenges you've faced.

When you're clear about the Big Picture, it's easier to stay motivated, even when you are faced with setbacks or challenges. Understanding the greater purpose behind your daily tasks can transform them from mundane to meaningful, and it can instill a sense of urgency and necessity in your actions.

Think about reverse engineering your Big Picture like this. Imagine the career or business you ultimately want to have:

- How does it look?
- With whom are you working?
- What kind of projects are you handling?
- How is your day-to-day life?

 **Blue Tip:** Enhance your daily motivation by creating a vision board that visually represents your goals and aspirations. Place it somewhere that you'll see it every day to keep your focus aligned with your ambitions and inspire continuous action towards your Big Picture.

Once you've got a clear picture of this ideal scenario, you begin working backwards from there. Break down what you need to achieve that end goal. Identify the skills, the network, the resources, and the steps you might need to get there. This approach helps you set up a clear pathway from where you are right now in your current, unsatisfying corporate role to where you want to be. It's about plotting your *Beautiful Exit* and subsequent journey with a strategic map, detailing every turn you need to take to reach your ultimate destination. By reverse engineering your career or business goals, **you're not just dreaming about a future; you're strategically planning how to make it your reality.**

To further enhance your *Beautiful Exit* from an unmatched corporate role into a fulfilling new chapter, whether as an entrepreneur or in another capacity, here are the three stages of the *Logistics of Purpose* and strategies to navigate them with momentum:

1. Idea Exploration

At this initial stage, your primary focus is to **shape your vision and set the foundation**:

The Loudness of Silence: When planning your next career move, especially if it involves leaving your current position, discretion is your ally. Be selective about whom you share your aspirations with in your workplace. You can't always predict how others might react or use the information about your plans to leave as motives can vary widely. Keeping your cards close to your chest not only protects your current professional standing, but it also empowers you to move on your terms when the time is right.

MAPP is Your Cheat Code

Mentors: Seek out experts who can offer not just guidance but also accelerated growth through their experiences and networks. Consider mentorship as "buying back your time" by learning from others' mistakes and successes.

> For example, if your end goal is to be a health and wellness consultant to educators, ideally you would seek a mentor(s) who worked directly in schools, educational administration, or in designing programs specifically for educators

Accountability Partners: These are the people who will keep you **consistent, motivated, and on track** towards your goals, giving you honest feedback as needed.

Peers: Engage with peers for emotional support, shared learning, and potential collaborations. They **enrich your journey** and provide a safety net during transitions.

Think of *creating your MAPP* as taking the elevator, not the stairs. You are choosing to work smarter, not harder. Each component—**Mentors, Accountability Partners, and Peers**—offers unique benefits that can *accelerate and elevate* your progress and enhance your capabilities. By aligning these relationships with your end goals, you ensure that every interaction and piece of advice received moves you closer to your Big Picture.

Linking your MAPP network to your future workspaces isn't just about leveraging these relationships for immediate benefits. It's about surrounding yourself with the community and culture of your chosen field, which can provide ongoing support, resources, and opportunities. This *strategic alignment* helps in building a relevant and supportive professional ecosystem around you.

— **Take a moment and identify three people in each category of your MAPP network who bring unique qualities to the table.** Aim to formalize these relationships within the next 30 days, whether that's through a mentorship request for a period of time or the establishment of clear intentions for mutual growth and support with an accountability partner or peer.

 **Blue Tip:** It's important to maintain your current connections while extending your network. Look to find a neutral ground where you can continue nurturing older, healthy relationships because they, too, can offer unexpected insights and support. This paves the way for a harmonious approach that respects your past while building toward your future.

2. Decision Point

At this pivotal moment, **saying "Yes to You"** becomes not just a decision, but an event. This stage is a significant, defining moment when you affirm your choice to pivot and confidently step forward on your new path. This is the culmination of your introspection and planning, marking the point where you fully commit to pursuing a new direction that perhaps few have dared to tread. It is the very essence of choosing a road less traveled, echoing the profound words of the author, Robert Frost:

> *"Two roads diverged in a wood, and I — I took the one less traveled by, And that has made all the difference."*

This point in time is about valuing your self-worth, often long neglected in the pursuit of conventional success. It's a powerful assertion of your values, your desires, and your potential. As you make this choice, it's crucial to:

Guard Your Duty of Discernment: Protect your journey by saying 'no' to distractions and commitments that do not align with your purpose. This discernment is vital as it helps you avoid paths that may lead you away from your chosen goals.

Practical Trumps Passion: While passion is a powerful initial motivator, it can diminish over time, especially when it is faced with challenges or routine tasks. It's essential to ground your career decisions in practicality to ensure their sustainability and long-term satisfaction.

In embracing this stage, you're not just making a change; you are redefining your trajectory in a way that aligns deeply with who you are and who you aspire to be.

3. Leading Steps

Strategic Prioritization: Focus on what is most important. Identify tasks that significantly impact your goals and allocate your resources accordingly.

- Ensures that your limited resources such as time, money, and effort are used more efficiently.
- Helps align daily tasks with long-term goals.
- Equips you to know that you are working on what is most important, *reducing anxiety and stress*. It creates a sense of control and accomplishment.

Focusing on the right tasks at the right time increases the quality of work and the likelihood of you achieving your desired results, whether it is in a project, a business, or your personal growth.

Deliberate Patience: Is not about inaction; it's about controlled action. It's knowing when to pause, when to proceed, and when to push harder, aligning your pace with the tempo of your environment and your objectives for maximum impact.

- When facing the urge to make hasty decisions, *you reduce risk*.
- You are more informed, and you make well-thought-out choices that are likely to *lead to better outcomes*.

Sometimes, the best action is in calculated waiting, allowing for the cultivation and maturation of opportunities that might not be immediately ready but could be highly beneficial in the long run.

Personal Branding and Social Proofing: This is the strategic process of shaping a distinct and cohesive professional identity and then reinforcing your identity with evidence and endorsements that validate your capabilities. Here's how it breaks down:

Revisit your personal capability statement: Define your "your special edge" in the market which highlights what makes you uniquely valuable in your professional field.

- *Consistent Messaging*: Ensure all your communications, from your digital profiles to your personal interactions, convey your brand consistently, reflecting your professional identity and values.

- *Utilize Online Platforms*: Leverage professional networking sites like LinkedIn to connect with industry leaders, join relevant groups, and participate in discussions that showcase your expertise and interests. Include endorsements from colleagues, clients, or mentors and ensure your achievements and skills are well documented and visible.

- *Content Creation and Sharing*: Share insights, write articles, or speak at industry events. These activities not only solidify your position as an emerging thought leader, but they also serve as direct social proof of your expertise

The long-term impact of maintaining a focus on both personal branding and social proof ensures control over your professional narrative. It allows you to actively manage how you are perceived in your industry, helping you navigate your career transition smoothly. Over time, your well-established brand and the social proof that supports it, contribute to the legacy you leave in your field, defining the influence and impact you have on others. This heavily supports your move to **CEO - Corporate to Entrepreneurship On your terms**

Network to Net Worth: As you build your personal brand, networking helps to amplify your presence in your industry. As an entrepreneur, the ability to connect with the right people at the right time can significantly propel your career forward.

Strategic networking goes beyond casual connections; it involves purposefully building relationships that are mutually beneficial and that directly support your long-term goals. Leverage it in ways that enhance your economic status and career trajectory. This involves:

- *Identify Key Influencers and Leaders*: Focus on connecting with individuals who are influential in your target market or industry.
- *Engage in Industry Events*: Attend conferences, seminars, and workshops relevant to your business.
- *Offer Value*: Always approach networking with a mindset of offering value. Whether it's sharing insights, providing support, or connecting others, ensure that your interactions are beneficial for both parties.

Repetition is Your Friend: As an entrepreneur, to go from good to great requires consistent actions. Consistency is a cornerstone of success for any entrepreneur, acting as the glue that holds all elements of your business strategy together. You will enhance your skills through regular practice and refinement, leading to mastery in your specific field. Establishing habits through consistent actions boosts both productivity and discipline, ensuring steady progress towards your goals even on less motivated days. To effectively implement consistency:

- *Develop a Routine* that integrates these tasks into your daily or weekly schedule, ensuring that each action is aligned with your *Big Picture*.
- *Monitoring and Measuring* these actions allows you to assess their effectiveness and make necessary adjustments. Actively seek feedback from current and potential clients, mentors, or peers to ensure that your consistent efforts are yielding the desired results.

Pitfalls of Desperation

During high-pressure situations, there is a natural inclination to act swiftly, often out of desperation. While speed is sometimes necessary, it's crucial to distinguish between being quick and being hasty. Being quick involves acting with efficiency and promptness, often after thoughtful planning, while being hasty means rushing through decisions without adequate consideration, potentially overlooking important details. Desperation can cloud your judgment, pushing you to make rushed decisions that might seem to solve immediate problems, but they fail to align with your long-term career goals.

You will have times as an entrepreneur, when making a critical decision requires quick, reactive responses. A measured response can be done with speed. I want to emphasize the importance of maintaining a level head and engaging in deliberate thinking, even in the face of urgency. Remain calm to avoid emotional or panicked reactions that can lead to poor decision-making. Here's how you can manage such situations:

- *Pause and Prioritize*: Even a brief pause can help you collect your thoughts and prioritize your actions based on what is most critical at the moment. Weigh the pros and cons of different options, considering the potential outcomes and impacts of each choice.
- *Connect with the Big Picture*: Before making any decision, quickly assess how the action fits within your broader career aspirations. Does it propel you forward, or could it potentially set you back?
- *Consult Quickly but Wisely*: If time permits, a quick consultation with a mentor or peer (your MAPP) can provide a fresh perspective or validation of your intended action.
- *Reflect on Past Experiences*: Draw on similar past experiences in which you've successfully navigated urgent decisions. What worked well? What didn't?

The Power of Preparedness

> *"Let your eyes look straight ahead; fix your gaze directly*
> *before you. Give careful thought to the paths for your feet*
> *and be steadfast in all your ways."*
> – Proverbs 4:25-26 NIV

Moves that matter are not just about taking action, but they are about *taking the right action at the right time*. This strategic plan and approach **minimize risks and maximizes outcomes**, ensuring that each step you take is a powerful stride toward your ultimate vision. Stay grounded in your vision. Let your Big Picture thinking guide you but remain flexible to adapt as circumstances evolve.

In navigating the complexities of establishing your livelihood, preparedness is your most valuable asset. It involves more than just foresight; it requires a comprehensive understanding of your goals, the obstacles you may face, and the resources at your disposal. This deep level of preparedness allows you to anticipate changes, prepare for potential challenges, and seize opportunities with precision. By doing so, you not only enhance your resilience, but you also ensure that your efforts are both effective and efficient.

As you move forward, it is crucial to integrate this strategic preparedness into every facet of your planning. Develop a mindset that values thorough analysis and detailed strategy over haste. Each decision and each action should be deliberate and informed, crafted to bring you closer to your envisioned future. Remember, the best-laid plans consider not only the destination but also the journey—including the unexpected detours.

While it's essential to be guided by your overarching vision— your Big Picture—it's equally important to maintain flexibility. The ability to adapt is a powerful skill in an ever-changing world market. Conditions change and new information emerges but being too rigid can be as detrimental to you as being unprepared.

Balancing steadfastness in your goals with adaptability in your methods is the key to navigating your path successfully.

Embrace the power of preparedness by meticulously planning, eagerly anticipating, and skillfully adjusting. Let your readiness empower each step you take, ensuring that every move is not just a step but a leap towards your aspirations. With preparedness as your foundation, you are more likely to navigate through your career and life not just with success, but with significance.

CHAPTER EIGHT

Unbalanced CHOICE

Embracing the harmony of work and life is to understand
that their priorities will trade places often.

B alancing your career ambitions with your personal life can feel like walking a tightrope. Every day, you face decisions that tug at your time and attention, pulling you in multiple directions. The Scale^2 method is designed to help you navigate the people, places, and circumstances that impact your choices by measuring their relevance and support. Use of this method will help you prioritize effectively, ensuring that each major decision aligns with your immediate needs and your ultimate vision.

While it is vital to plan for the future, living in and appreciating the 'now' is crucial. Ignoring the present can lead to burnout and a loss of motivation, so it is important to engage fully with your current activities while keeping your future goals in mind.

Entrepreneurship often demands intense bursts of activity—what we can think of as *seasonal sprints*. These sprints are times when you push hard to launch new products, reach new markets, or achieve significant milestones. Just as important are your periods of rest which should be in rotation with your sprints. Your *rest periods* are essential for reflection, recovery, and strategic planning, allowing you to renew your energy and prepare for the next push.

Your journey of entrepreneurship should not be constant acceleration but rather a balanced cycle of sprints and pauses. This approach allows you to stay grounded in the present, attending to your well-being while also driving your business forward. Take note that valuing the 'now' does not mean losing sight of the future; instead, it enhances your ability to approach your work with a clear mind and a healthy perspective, making your entrepreneurial endeavors both sustainable and more purpose-filled.

The Scale^2 Method

Imagine having a tool that quickly tells you how well a person, place, or project supports your growth and purpose. That is what Scale^2 does. It is a dual-criteria method developed to help you weigh your options in the context of your long-term benefits and immediate relevance. The Scale^2 method empowers you to make a **CHOICE** that aligns with you professionally and personally based on *factors* (people, places, and things) that are the heaviest consumers of your time, resources, and mental capacities.

Choose: Selecting options that resonate with your goals.

How: Determining the approach or strategy that best suits your needs.

Opportunity: Identifying chances for advancement and growth.

Impact: Assessing the potential effects on your lifestyle.

Career and Life: Balancing the demands and rewards of both.

Execute: Putting your decisions into action effectively.

The Scale^2 method incorporates several key components that are essential for navigating both the immediate and long-range challenges of your entrepreneurial journey. Each component plays a critical role in ensuring that your actions are both effective and strategically aligned with your overarching goals. This method serves as a strategic tool to help you evaluate and prioritize the factors that affect your decision making, based on their capacity to support your growth and purpose.

Consider your purpose in entrepreneurship to be like an *Oak Tree*:

This grand and sturdy tree, when fully grown, represents the fulfillment of your career and personal dreams. Your entrepreneurial path, much like the life cycle of an oak tree, starts with a fundamental seed — your core purpose that fuels all your initiatives. As this seed germinates and grows, transforming from a delicate sprout into a robust oak, your business or career evolves, and it is shaped and sustained by crucial elements that are akin to the nurturing forces of nature such as sunlight, soil, and water. These factors provide the necessary support and environment for the oak to thrive just as strategic decisions and resources foster the development and success of your entrepreneurial endeavors.

Pillars of Success

Entrepreneurial Agility: As you navigate the changing landscapes of your industry, your ability to adapt is crucial. *How quickly can you pivot your strategies to seize new opportunities?* Agility ensures that your role and business remain competitive and resilient in a constantly evolving marketplace.

Delegation for Acceleration: Think about the tasks you currently handle. Which of these could be delegated? Effective delegation isn't just about freeing up your time; it's about empowering others and enhancing your focus on areas that require your unique skills. Your willingness to delegate is fundamental to scaling any venture. Delegating tasks allows you to *accelerate your business's growth and elevate its reach* by freeing up your time to focus on high-impact activities and strategic planning.

Enhancing Relevant Skill Keys: Identifying and developing the skill keys you currently possess that support both your short-term and long-term goals is vital, and it *streamlines your efforts*. These skills could range from technical abilities specific to your industry to soft skills like leadership and communication, which are critical for managing growth and navigating business challenges.

Analyzing Resource Allocation: A crucial question you face is whether *you have more money than time or more time than money*. Understanding this balance acts as a tipping point, guiding you on how to allocate your resources efficiently. This is a key piece in forecasting and budgeting, helping you to prioritize investments in time or money based on your current situation and future goals.

Tipping the Scale

Let's put Scale[2] into practice. Select 3 to 5 factors [people, place, or project] that significantly influence and impact your career planning and development. Rate each factor on their support for growth and purpose using the following questions. Rate each factor on a scale from 1 to 5 [Access the downloadable template at choiceblueprint.com]

1 **Not Supportive**: Offers little to no support.
2 **Minimally Supportive**: Shows limited support, providing some benefits but not enough to significantly influence.
3 **Neutral**: Neither significantly supports nor hinders; it does not play a decisive role.
4 **Supportive**: Actively contributes, providing noticeable benefits and support.
5 **Highly Supportive**: Highest level of support. It greatly enhances and actively drives growth.

1. To what extent does this factor contribute to your professional growth?
2. How closely is this factor aligned with your core purpose?
3. Does this factor improve your ability to delegate tasks and responsibilities effectively?
4. Does this enhance your ability to adapt swiftly and effectively to market changes and opportunities?
5. How effectively does this factor help you balance and allocate your resources, specifically your time and finances?

After rating, sum up the score of each factor and classify them into one of the following ranges:

1-8: Unaligned This range suggests that most elements are not supporting your growth and purpose effectively. Factors falling in this category are likely detracting from your goals and may require significant changes or elimination from your strategies.

9-18: Needs Revision Scores in this range indicate that while there are some supportive elements, there is room for improvement. Revisions may be necessary to better align these factors with your goals. This might involve increasing the level of support or reassessing the importance of certain elements.

19-25: Big Picture Worthy This is the ideal range, indicating that the majority of factors are highly supportive of your growth and purpose. Elements in this category are well-aligned with your overarching goals and are effectively driving your progress.

Using the Scale² method thoughtfully by selecting no more than five factors to focus on can significantly enhance the quality and effectiveness of your ability to apply this in a relevant, result producing manner. By limiting your focus to a manageable number of key elements, you *avoid the common pitfall of multitasking to a fault*, which often leads to diluted efforts and diminished outcomes. Concentrating on a few chosen factors allows you to invest deeper thought and more substantial effort into each one, ensuring that you are not just ticking boxes but actually engaging with each aspect in a meaningful way.

This targeted approach helps you maintain a clear and focused strategy, making it easier to measure progress and adjust tactics as necessary. It also *reduces the cognitive load and decision fatigue that come with juggling too many variables*, allowing you to stay more organized and less stressed. You will find that dedicating sufficient time and resources to these select factors not only optimizes your outcomes, but it also accelerates your progress toward your goals.

By filtering and simplifying your priorities, you're able to delve into the nuances and complexities of each, fostering a richer understanding and more effective implementation of strategies that drive real, tangible growth. Remember, *sometimes, less is more*, and in the context of your career development, this focused approach can yield significantly better results than spreading yourself too thin.

It's a Celebration

In the midst of navigating your career transition and embracing the pivotal decisions that shape your journey, it is vital to cultivate an "**Attitude of Gratitude**." This mindset isn't just about feeling thankful in a general sense; it's about deeply appreciating and recognizing your own agency. Celebrate and honor your freedom to choose and your power to pivot today, setting the tone for your leading steps. **The freedom of decision making that you possess today is a privilege**. Celebrating these capabilities enriches your path and profoundly impacts your approach to leadership and personal growth.

Gratitude can clear your mind for better decision-making, and each choice can be made with clarity and less anxiety. It builds resilience by helping you recognize and appreciate past challenges you've overcome and lessons you've learned, boosting your confidence for future hurdles. This mindset also enhances your leadership qualities, fostering empathy and humility, which are essential for motivating and engaging teams.

Acknowledging the contributions of your mentors, peers, and team members strengthens your professional relationships, promoting a collaborative and supportive work environment. Furthermore, gratitude increases personal satisfaction, allowing you to enjoy greater contentment in your career, which fuels ongoing development.

Cultivating a culture of thankfulness within your workspaces can transform the environment, making it more positive and reducing competitive tensions. It encourages innovation, efficiency, and collective success. Additionally, the practice of gratitude creates a positive feedback loop, enhancing your responsiveness to the positives in your environment and encouraging kind actions towards others.

As you move toward your Big Picture, reflect on the internal and external factors that have equipped you with the courage to take confident steps at this critical juncture in your life. Consider the choices you've made, the flexibility you've exercised, and the people who have supported your journey. This not only grounds your actions and intentions, but it also enriches your professional demeanor and reputation.

In celebrating your ability to make pivotal decisions, you reinforce your readiness to direct your career's future with a balanced, grateful, and confident outlook. You are grounding your actions and intentions in a worldview that not only appreciates what has been, but it also optimistically anticipates what is yet to come. An *attitude of gratitude* is not merely an exercise in thankfulness; it is a well-rounded approach that enhances your professional growth. By acknowledging and celebrating your power of **CHOICE** and your ability to pivot, you reinforce your readiness to embrace and direct the future of your career with gratitude, humility, and confidence.

DESTINATIONS

7

6

5 Power

4 Picture

3 Purpose

2 Path

1 Process

CHOICE

PART FOUR

CHOICE

CHAPTER NINE

Fat Elephant

What's the fastest way to eat an elephant?
One bite at a time!

Just like with any monumental task, achieving greatness isn't about doing the average; it's about answering your calling to lead, embracing the challenge, breaking it down into manageable pieces, and conquering each step with determination and excellence. Remember, you were not born to be average; you were meant to walk the less traveled paths and excel beyond the ordinary. The return on your investment that comes with risks and challenges will yield high rewards in your new way of life, and **you will thrive.**

Your newfound success will lead to your deserved and authentic reputation, preceding you in new spaces with new faces. Your fat elephant presence will validate your spirit of entrepreneurship in all the rooms you enter. The fat elephant exit from your corporate anxiety is to be surrounded with your *pillars of* **PEACE** [detailed in chapter 6].

P – Planned Your Beautiful Exit
E - Expanded Your Skill Keys
A - Assessed Your Corporate Currency
C - Committed to Continuous Learning
E - Embraced Change and Adaptability

Answering the Entrepreneurial Call

The term "entrepreneurial spirit" has become a trendy and an overused mantra. The mainstream, uninformed desire to start a business based on their limited perception of success versus the reality of what it takes to be a success is the reason nearly half of new businesses fail within 5 years. It is through the experience lens of my own entrepreneurship ventures and corporate path that I can testify to the calling of purpose through entrepreneurship and the connection it has to sustainability. I managed to elevate and accelerate in various roles throughout my career. I moved from an independent beauty advisor and stylist to a career educator to administrator to director. In less than 3 years, I transitioned from an inside sales rep to a senior account executive, overseeing million-dollar logistics contracts.

When you are…
> *Creating* your story
> *Identifying* your value
> *Cultivating* your power to grow
> *Choosing* your terms

…you are aware *"the opportunity to choose is our strength and freedom"* - Joseph Murphy

The **Fat Elephant Entrepreneur** is a visionary adept at navigating both corporate and entrepreneurial terrains with exceptional agility and foresight. Dr. Joseph Murphy, the author of *The Power of Your Subconscious Mind* encapsulates this with his viewpoint, *"Age is not the flight of years; it is the dawn of wisdom."* The transformation of years of experience, including corporate challenges, into valuable triumphs and fresh starts is the essence of a Fat Elephant Entrepreneur. As strong leaders, they repeatedly embrace strategic vulnerability and conduct intentional branding. The pivot payoff is big for the Fat Elephant Entrepreneur.

Unapologetic Vision

In a world where shortcuts and compromises might sometimes seem like the easier route, embracing integrity is not just a choice but a fundamental aspect of a successful and sustainable lifestyle. Integral integrity paves the way for having an *unapologetic vision*—a **clear, confident path forward that requires no**

justification and is a foundation for trustworthiness and authenticity in all aspects of life.

When you consistently align your words with your actions and maintain your standards even in challenging situations, you cultivate a vision for your life and work that stands uncompromised. This integrity-driven vision enables you to be bold and assertive in your pursuits. You don't have to apologize for your ambitions or the paths you choose because each step you take resonates with your ethical and moral compass. When you move with integrity, you naturally develop a vision for your life and work that you can stand behind without reservation. This connection between your values and actions not only fosters a deep sense of purpose and direction within yourself, but it also inspires those around you.

The path of integrity may not always be the simplest, but it is unquestionably the most fulfilling. Embrace this path, and you will find that living and working with an unapologetic vision is not just possible, but it is profoundly rewarding.

With the *audacity of vision*, the Fat Elephant Entrepreneur does not seek permission to pursue their dreams. They face obstacles head-on and make today's moments pivotal for their future success. Their approach from corporate to entrepreneurship is rooted in a deep understanding of their *corporate currency*—the "what" they bring to the table. They are calculating risks and creating plans for business ventures that the open, global market needs. Their entrepreneurial journey is continuously fueled by a purpose that aligns with their Personal Vault and Big Picture.

Fat Elephant audacity is to operate in the present with conviction to being called to not just navigate but shape the landscape of your professional life with strategic acumen and a profound sense of purpose. Your "one bite at time" could be:

- Celebrating small wins while understanding their compounding effects to keep you pushing forward.
- Scheduling sprints and rest periods to distribute good energetic contributions to your well-being.
- Planning for short-term needs while investing in your long-term goals.

I remember having "on the record" (annual performance reviews) and candid conversations with one of my favorite managers and mentors regarding my next steps in the organization. When I would talk about my salary goals, he would often say, "Chase the career, and the money will follow." Within my tenure with that company, I received three sought-after promotions within a span of fewer than 4 years and enjoyed a company expense paid relocation to a city where I had always wanted to move. My salary increased by 177% (about 32% each year). Please note that typical annual American corporate salary raises are often in the average range of 3% to 5% under normal economic conditions. His advice paid off big.

The Business of People

In all their endeavors, Fat Elephant Entrepreneurs embody Maya Angelou's famous sentiment:

> *"People will forget what you said, people will forget what you did, but people will never forget how you made them feel."*

You may ask, "What does that quote have to do with money?"

Strong relationships drive business. When people feel valued and respected, they are more likely to become loyal customers, recommend your services to others, and choose your business over competitors. This loyalty and advocacy can translate into increased revenue and growth for your business.

Retaining good teams and talent. How you make your team and employees feel directly impacts their motivation, productivity, and loyalty to your company. *Happy people are more engaged and productive,* which can lead to better business outcomes and reduced costs associated with high turnover.

Expanding horizons to create diverse opportunities. *Your biggest asset truly is people.* Building a diverse network can be key in creating multiple streams of income by way of cross-industry innovation and risk diversification. Diverse perspectives lead the way for creating solutions that can be monetized in various ways such as consulting services, partnerships, or even joint ventures.

People prefer to do business with those who make them feel heard and appreciated, which can lead to more favorable financial terms.

Creating positive emotional connections and demonstrating genuine appreciation in business relationships can significantly enhance financial outcomes. By connecting with a broad range of people, you open doors to a variety of income-generating projects that might not have been accessible otherwise. When people feel valued, they are more likely to offer more advantageous terms and opportunities. Your branding efforts produce positive perceptions among stakeholders that can boost your market value, attract investors, and improve negotiating power.

Your Money Plan

Pursue profitability through solutions that are in global market demands.

That's it! Simply solve a problem. Identify and market to the people who have and will pay money to fix their problem.

The inner workings of your revenue goals should show up through your business planning stages (again, I will let the financial planners do the heavy lifting here). However, the measuring and adjusting of your business milestones and key performance indicators (KPIs) must be a constant process throughout your journey as the visionary leader. If you do not know how to set these, find someone quickly in your industry who does. You cannot fix what you don't know is a problem. You must keep a watchful eye, using data-driven metrics, to know how your business is performing.

Regarding setting financial goals, the easiest way to take "*one bite at a time*" is to use your time as the metric. In chapter 7, we discussed the process of reverse engineering to develop a tangible plan to achieve your Big Picture. Planning and starting with an end in mind is relevant here too. For example, to achieve a net income of $100,000 within a year, a structured timeline and a clear set of financial targets can guide you effectively. Here's an example how you can break down this goal into manageable segments:

Goal: Achieve a net income of $100,000
Time Frame: 1 Year

Step 1: Quarterly Breakdown
Your annual goal is divided into four equal quarterly targets to streamline your focus and financial planning (seasonal scenario for sales highest in summer months)

Q1 Goal: $15,000
Q2 Goal: $25,000
Q3 Goal: $35,000 capitalizing on peak summer sales
Q4 Goal: $25,000 adjusting for the post-summer dip and pre-holiday sales

Step 2: Set Your Monthly Targets

Each quarterly goal is further divided into three months, making it easier to monitor and adjust strategies as needed:

Months 1-3: Each month aim to net $5,000
Months 4-6: Each month targets $8,333
Months 7-9: $11,667 each month, making the most of the summer sales spike
Months 10-12: Each month secure $8,333

Step 3: Weekly Actions are adjusted based on the monthly goal. They are typically divided by four weeks, ensuring that each week's efforts contribute effectively towards the monthly and quarterly targets.

Milestones and Key Performance Indicators (KPIs):

- Evaluate the quarterly income. Reassess your strategies and plan for the next quarter.

- Monthly KPIs: Number of sales, conversion rates, client acquisition and retention, operational efficiencies.

By dissecting your annual goal into quarterly, monthly, and weekly bites, you will more effectively manage activities and ensure steady progress towards your overall financial target.

Spiritual Ground

The Fat Elephant Entrepreneur spiritual foundation is deeply rooted in resilience, wisdom, and a distinct sense of purpose. I personally draw inspiration from Biblical teachings in James 1:12. It says, *"They exemplify perseverance and steadfastness, embodying grace as they navigate life's trials."* Fat Elephant Entrepreneurs recognize that wisdom accumulates not merely with age, but it accrues through the varied experiences and lessons life imparts. They cherish the community around them, viewing their network as more than just a business tool. It is a source of spiritual support and connectivity, fostering relationships that are both giving and nurturing. Your spiritual ground lays the foundation that guides you through the complexities of entrepreneurship, and it enriches your interactions, instilling CPR – *clarity, purpose, and resilience* to your work and life with a meaningful and purpose-driven approach to business.

At the core of your spiritual essence should be your clear sense of purpose that transcends mere financial gains. Your business endeavors are an extension of your larger calling or mission that resonate deeply with your personal values. A Fat Elephant Entrepreneur approaches their successes with a recognition of larger forces at play. They are grateful for the opportunities and their achievements and humble about their role that lies within them.

Harnessing the breadth and design of Fat Elephant energy captures and acknowledges the sheer scale and depth of your effort and determination required to transform big visions to your reality. Fat Elephant energy itself symbolizes the power and impact of your efforts—one bite at a time.

"What you get by achieving your goals is not as important as what you become by achieving your goal."

– John Maxwell

CHAPTER TEN

Piece to Peace

It is my highest hope that you understand the
intention of this book is to
Build You, Before you Build your Business.

This "Piece to Peace" blueprint to *Shift from Corporate Surviving to Entrepreneurial Thriving* encapsulates the essence of your transformative journey upon which you have embarked. It's about making your Fat Elephant entrance to new beginnings, forming the bedrock of your work and lifestyle stance. Your Beautiful Exit from the corporate world initiates the path to your big dreams and overarching Big Picture.

One of the key lessons to carry forward is the understanding that when you attempt to be everything for everyone, your impact is inevitably diminished. Your focused efforts and targeted goals are about honing in on what truly matters. Your decision to design your career path in purpose (true design), on purpose (with intent), and with purpose (aligned to core beliefs) highlights a critical transformative starting point. This strategic approach ensures that fear no longer serves as an obstacle. You have embraced a life in which your decisions are deliberate, your actions are impactful, and your path is unequivocally yours. Your self-promised vision of worthiness is the driving force behind the perseverance that will help keep you on track for success.

You have learned how to redefine your identity, recognize your true value and how to apply it, and harness your visionary power to carve out your desired destination. This process has unlocked the unlimited potential of this blueprint, setting the stage for you to confidently navigate towards your aspirations. You have learned that while the journey is not without challenges, the clarity of your vision and the peace of mind that comes from living in the present and trusting your personal compass, serve as your steadfast guides.

The Power to Reboot

"When the mind has a defined target, it can focus and direct and refocus and redirect until it reaches its intended goal."
– Tony Robbins

Holding your Big Picture in mind equips you with the powerful ability to reboot or execute the **Control/Alt/Delete** command on your life's approach:

- **Control** What Can Be Controlled: *Focus your energy on what is within your power* and learn to let go of what isn't. This mindset helps maintain your mental energy and keeps you steadfast on your journey.
- Consider **Alternative** and Non-Traditional Ideas: Innovation doesn't follow a popular path. *Embrace ideas that are impactful over those that are merely popular,* allowing for creative solutions that challenge the status quo.
- **Delete** Negativity: Purge negative influences—people, places, and habits—that do not support your journey [use case for Scale^2]. This cleansing allows you to maintain a clear focus on your path forward, *ensuring that only those who can contribute positively accompany you.*

It is crucial to carry forward the profound sense of renewal and readiness. *The Choice Destinations P7 Blueprint* isn't merely a sequence of steps; it is the framework upon which you will build a life and career that are not only successful but are also profoundly fulfilling. Remember, each choice you make, informed by your true self and aimed at your ultimate objectives, is not just a step towards achieving your goals; it is a manifestation of the peace and alignment you have cultivated through your journey. "Piece to Peace" marks a significant shift. It is both a reflection of all you've learned and a guide for the continued application of these principles, ensuring that the path you design is as rewarding as the destinations you aim to reach.

Choice Destinations P7 Blueprint: Putting the Pieces Together

1. PROCESS

When facing the pivotal decision of whether to stay in your current role or pivot to a more purposeful position, you start by thoroughly assessing your current career and business situation. Reflecting deeply on your personal satisfaction, the alignment of your current role with your values, and the growth opportunities it presents is crucial for understanding the breadth and depth of the challenge ahead.

- This is the PROCESS in which you establish the foundation of your decision-making framework by critically evaluating where you stand and where you want to go.

2. PATH

Next, gather as much information as possible about the potential new role or direction. This might involve conducting market research, consulting with mentors, and networking with peers who have embarked on similar transitions. This information will guide your strategic decisions, helping you map out the path ahead.

- The PATH is defined by the idea exploration stage in which you explore potential routes and prepare for the journey ahead based on informed decisions.

3. PURPOSE

With a clear understanding of the landscape, carefully weigh the risks and benefits of making a career pivot versus staying in your current role. Consider the financial implications, personal life impact, and the long-term benefits of aligning your career more closely with your purpose.

- PURPOSE is reaffirmed here as you align your career goals with your deeper life values, ensuring that your actions are driven by meaningful objectives.

4. PICTURE

Seeking advice from trusted advisors or mentors is also a vital step. Their outside perspective can provide invaluable insights, helping you to see things you might overlook and affirming whether your planned pivot aligns with your long-term objectives.

- The big PICTURE becomes clearer as you consult with mentors and advisors, helping you visualize the potential outcomes and refine your vision.

5. POWER

Should you decide to pivot, plan your transition meticulously. Outline clear goals, establish realistic timelines, and identify the resources you'll need. Each step of your plan should be designed to ensure a smooth transition (Beautiful Exit), making the process manageable and aligned with your ultimate goals.

- POWER is harnessed through careful planning and resource allocation, empowering you to execute your Big Picture effectively.

6. PERSEVERANCE

Begin implementing your transition plan incrementally. Approach each step thoughtfully, ensuring that every action contributes positively towards your new direction. Maintain flexibility throughout this process and be ready to adjust your plan as new information and circumstances warrant.

- PERSEVERANCE is demonstrated as you begin to enact your plan, facing challenges and adapting as necessary while steadfastly moving toward your goals.

7. PEACE

Finally, continuously evaluate your progress toward your new goals. Regular check-ins and adjustments to your plan are essential, ensuring that each step you take is not only deliberate but also effective in moving you closer to a more fulfilling and purpose-driven career.

- PEACE is achieved through ongoing evaluation and adaptation, ensuring that each *piece* of your plan contributes to a serene transition, which ultimately will lead to a career that is more aligned with your aspirations and true self.

The Choice Destinations P7 Blueprint designs a barrier breaking path to your destination of peace and fulfillment in every piece of your professional mosaic.

When my position was dissolved as a six-figure earning, top performing executive, the writing had long been written on the walls that I was operating outside of my purpose-led life. I was burned-out beyond capacity, and I had lost sight of the joy I had once had as an early entrepreneur. I understood then that money can be a facilitator of happiness, but it was never my true source. I made the **CHOICE** to piece together my **CEO - Corporate to Entrepreneurship On my terms** mindset.

The plan of thoughts and actions outlined throughout this book will lead you to a place of **deliverance, intention, and courage** that will allow you to experience a sense of peace and allow you to rejoice, holding a bouquet of lessons learned, achievements met, and embracement of the unknown. From the origin and revelation of your **I Am** identity, you created your guiding **Big Picture** that your *personal compass* will help you navigate to. The sum of your *why's, skill keys, corporate currency, and pillars of PEACE* are now woven in your *personal capability statement.* You are hyper-intentional about protecting your *ecosystem,* and you use your **M.A.P.P** as a cheat code to elevate and expedite your new path to becoming a **Fat Elephant Entrepreneur.** The **Scale²** method should continue to be a measure and filter your choices as you gear up for any necessary career moves that matter, utilizing your *logistics of purpose.*

DESTINATIONS

7 Peace

6 Perseverance

5 Power

4 Picture

3 Purpose

2 Path

1 Process

CHOICE

DESTINATIONS

*"You can't add days to your life, but you can add life to
your days."* – unknown

Destinations may seem elusive because in this text, they represent not just a single endpoint. They represent a series of evolving goals and milestones throughout your life's journey. Achieving work-life harmony is about embracing the many paths and directions your life might take, each offering its own lessons and opportunities.

As you reflect on the insights gathered through these pages, remember that your journey doesn't culminate at a fixed point. Instead, think of each destination as a marker in a broader exploration of who you are and what you can accomplish. The paths you choose will shift and change, and they are influenced by your decisions, experiences, and the evolving equilibrium between your professional and personal life.

As you move forward, take comfort in knowing that the true essence of your journey lies not in reaching a final destination. It lies in the richness of the experiences you gather along the way. Embrace each phase with openness and curiosity, allowing your understanding of work-life harmony to deepen and expand. This is your journey, unique and full of potential; savor its every twist and turn. Keep exploring and let your path be a testament to your enduring spirit of discovery and self-realization as you *GROW through what you GO through.*

"May God bless you and be present in your future choices to your new destinations." – Jraya Nicole